Nathan Walworth, Peter Seddon, John Samuel Fletcher

The Correspondence of Nathan Walworth and Peter Seddon of

Outwood

And Other Documents Chiefly Relating to the Building of Ringley Chapel

Nathan Walworth, Peter Seddon, John Samuel Fletcher

The Correspondence of Nathan Walworth and Peter Seddon of Outwood
And Other Documents Chiefly Relating to the Building of Ringley Chapel

ISBN/EAN: 9783337425296

Printed in Europe, USA, Canada, Australia, Japan

Cover: Foto ©Suzi / pixelio.de

More available books at **www.hansebooks.com**

Chetham Society,

ESTABLISHED   M.DCCC.XLIII.

FOR THE PUBLICATION OF

HISTORICAL AND LITERARY REMAINS
CONNECTED WITH THE PALATINE COUNTIES OF
LANCASTER AND CHESTER.

Council for the year 1879-80.

President.
JAMES CROSSLEY, Esq., F.S.A.

Vice-President.
WILLIAM BEAMONT, Esq.

Council.
JOHN E. BAILEY, Esq., F.S.A.
The Very Rev. BENJAMIN MORGAN COWIE, D.D., F.S.A., Dean of Manchester
The Worshipful RICHARD COPLEY CHRISTIE, M.A., Chancellor of the Diocese
    of Manchester.
J. P. EARWAKER, Esq., M.A., F.S.A.,
LIEUT.-COLONEL FISHWICK, F.S.A.
HENRY H. HOWORTH, Esq., F.S.A.
WILLIAM LANGTON, Esq.
The Rev. JOHN HOWARD MARSDEN, B.D., F.R.G.S., late Disney Professor.
The Rev. JAMES RAINE, M.A., Canon of York, Fellow of Durham University.
FRANK RENAUD, Esq., M.D., F.S.A.

Treasurer.
ARTHUR H. HEYWOOD, Esq.

Honorary Secretary.
R. HENRY WOOD, Esq., F.S.A., F.R.G.S.,
Mem. Corr. Soc. Antiq. de Normandie.

RULES OF THE CHETHAM SOCIETY

1. That the Society shall be limited to three hundred and fifty members.
2. That the Society shall consist of members being subscribers of one pound annually, such subscription to be paid in advance, on or before the day of general meeting in each year. The first general meeting to be held on the 23rd day of March, 1843, and the general meeting in each year afterwards on the 1st day of March, unless it should fall on a Sunday, when some other day is to be named by the Council.
3. That the affairs of the Society be conducted by a Council, consisting of a permanent President and Vice-President, and twelve other members, including a Treasurer and Secretary, all of whom shall be elected, the first two at the general meeting next after a vacancy shall occur, and the twelve other members at the general meeting annually.
4. That the accounts of the receipts and expenditure of the Society be audited annually, by three auditors, to be elected at the general meeting; and that any member who shall be one year in arrear of his subscription, shall no longer be considered as belonging to the Society.
5. That every member not in arrear of his annual subscription, be entitled to a copy of each of the works published by the Society.
6. That twenty copies of each work shall be allowed to the editor of the same, in addition to the one to which he may be entitled as a member.

Applications and communications to be addressed to the PRESIDENT, *Stocks House, Cheetham, Manchester, or to the* HONORARY SECRETARY, *Penrhos House, Rugby.*

PUBLICATIONS OF THE CHETHAM SOCIETY.

Fourteenth year (1856–7).

VOL.

XL. The Private Journal and Literary Remains of John Byrom. Vol. II. Part I. *pp.* 326 *and two Indexes.*

XLI. The House and Farm Accounts of the Shuttleworths of Gawthorpe Hall. Part II. *pp.* 233–472. *Portrait.*

XLII. A History of the Ancient Chapels of Didsbury and Chorlton, in Manchester Parish, including Sketches of the Townships of Didsbury, Withington, Burnage, Heaton Norris, Reddish, Levenshulme, and Chorlton-cum-Hardy: together with Notices of the more Ancient Local Families, and Particulars relating to the Descent of their Estates. By the Rev. JOHN BOOKER, M.A., F.S.A. *pp.* viii, 337. *Seven Illustrations.*

Fifteenth year (1857–8).

XLIII. The House and Farm Accounts of the Shuttleworths of Gawthorpe Hall. Part III. *pp.* x, 473–776.

XLIV. The Private Journal and Literary Remains of John Byrom. Vol. II. Part II. *pp.* 327–654. *Byrom Pedigrees, pp.* 41 *and three folding sheets; Index, pp.* v.

XLV. Miscellanies: being a selection from the Poems and Correspondence of the Rev. Thos. Wilson, B.D., of Clitheroe. With Memoirs of his Life. By the Rev. CANON RAINES, M.A., F.S.A. *pp.* xc, 230. *Two Plates.*

Sixteenth year (1858–9).

XLVI. The House and Farm Accounts of the Shuttleworths of Gawthorpe Hall. Part IV. *(Conclusion). pp.* 777–1171.

XLVII. A History of the Ancient Chapel of Birch, in Manchester Parish, including a Sketch of the Township of Rusholme: together with Notices of the more Ancient Local Families, and Particulars relating to the Descent of their Estates. By the Rev. JOHN BOOKER, M.A., F.S.A. *pp.* viii, 255. *Four Plates.*

XLVIII. A Catalogue of the Collection of Tracts for and against Popery (published in or about the reign of James II.) in the Manchester Library founded by Humphrey Chetham; in which is incorporated, with large Additions and Bibliographical Notes, the whole of Peck's List of the Tracts in that Controversy, with his References. Edited by THOMAS JONES, Esq. B.A. Part I. *pp.* xii, 256.

Seventeenth year (1859–60).

XLIX. The Lancashire Lieutenancy under the Tudors and Stuarts. The Civil and Military Government of the County, as illustrated by a series of Royal and other Letters; Orders of the Privy Council, the Lord Lieutenant, and other Authorities, &c., &c. Chiefly derived from the Shuttleworth MSS. at Gawthorpe Hall, Lancashire. Edited by JOHN HARLAND, Esq., F.S.A. Part I. *pp.* cxx, 96. *Seven Plates.*

L. The Lancashire Lieutenancy under the Tudors and Stuarts. Part II. *(Conclusion). pp.* 97–333.

LI. Lancashire and Cheshire Wills and Inventories from the Ecclesiastical Court, Chester. The Second Portion. *pp.* vi, 283.

Eighteenth year (1860–1).

LII. Collectanea Anglo-Poetica: or, A Bibliographical and Descriptive Catalogue of a portion of a Collection of Early English Poetry, with occasional Extracts and Remarks Biographical and Critical. By the Rev. THOMAS CORSER, M.A., F.S.A., Rural Dean; Rector of Stand, Lancashire; and Vicar of Norton, Northamptonshire. Part I. *pp.* xi, 208.

LIII. Mamecestre: being Chapters from the early recorded History of the Barony, the Lordship or Manor, the Vill Borough or Town, of Manchester. Edited by JOHN HARLAND, Esq., F.S.A. Vol. I. *pp.* 207. *Frontispiece.*

LIV. Lancashire and Cheshire Wills and Inventories from the Ecclesiastical Court, Chester. The Third Portion. *(Conclusion). pp.* v, 272.

Nineteenth year (1861–2).

LV. Collectanea Anglo-Poetica. Part II. *pp.* vi, 209–456.

LVI. Mamecestre. Vol. II. *pp.* 209–431.

LVII. Chetham Miscellanies. Vol. III. Edited by WILLIAM LANGTON, Esq.: containing
On the South Lancashire Dialect, with Biographical Notices of John Collier, the author of *Tim Bobbin.* By THOS. HEYWOOD, Esq. *pp.* 84
Rentale de Cokersand: being the Bursar's Rent Roll of the Abbey of Cokersand, in the County Palatine of Lancaster, for the year 1501. Printed from the Original. Edited by the Rev. F. R. RAINES, M.A., F.S.A. *pp.* xviii, 46.

VOL.
The Names of all the Gentlemen of the best callinge wthin the countye of Lancastre, whereof choyse
ys to be made of a c'ten number to lend vnto her Ma^{ye} moneye vpon privie seals in Janvarye 1588.
From a manuscript in the possession of the Rev. F. R. RAINES, M.A., F.S.A. *pp.* 9.

Some Instruction given by William Booth Esquire to his stewards John Carington and William
Rowcrofte, upon the purchase of Warrington by Sir George Booth Baronet and William Booth his
son, A.D. MDCXVIII. Communicated by WILLIAM BEAMONT, Esq. *pp.* 8.

Letter from Sir John Seton, Manchester ye 25 M'ch, 1643. Edited by THOMAS HEYWOOD, Esq.,
F.S.A. *pp.* 15.

The Names of eight hundred inhabitants of Manchester who took the oath of allegiance to Charles
II. in April, 1679. Communicated by JOHN HARLAND, F.S.A. *pp.* 8.

The Pole Booke of Manchester, May ye 22^d 1690. Edited by WILLIAM LANGTON, Esq. *pp.* 43.
Map and folding Table.

Twentieth year (1862–3).

LVIII. Mamecestre. Vol. III. *(Conclusion.)* *pp.* xl, 433–627.
LIX. A History of the Chantries within the County Palatine of Lancaster : being the Reports of the
Royal Commissioners of Henry VIII., Edward VI., and Queen Mary. Edited by the Rev. F. R.
RAINES, M.A., F.S.A. Vol. I. *pp.* xxxix, 168.
LX. A History of the Chantries within the County Palatine of Lancaster, &c. Vol. II. *(Conclusion).*
pp. 169–323.

Twenty-first year (1863–4).

General Index to the Remains Historical and Literary published by the Chetham Society, vols. I-XXX.
pp. viii, 168.
LXI. 1. Abbott's Journal. II. An Account of the Tryalls &c. in Manchester in 1694. Edited by the
Rt. Rev. ALEXANDER GOSS, D.D. *pp.* xix, 32 ; xxi, 42 ; 5.
LXII. Discourse of the Warr in Lancashire. Edited by WILLIAM BEAMONT, Esq. *pp.* xxxiv, 164.
Two Plates.

Twenty-second year (1864–5).

LXIII. A Volume of Court Leet Records of the Manor of Manchester in the Sixteenth Century.
Compiled and edited by JOHN HARLAND, F.S.A. *pp.* xix, 208. *Frontispiece.*
LXIV. A Catalogue of the Collection of Tracts for and against Popery. Part II. To which are added
an Index to the Tracts in both editions of Gibson's Preservative, and a reprint of Dodd's Certamen,
Utriusque Ecclesiæ. Edited by THOMAS JONES, Esq., B.A. *pp.* x, 269, 17.
LXV. Continuation of the Court Leet Records of the Manor of Manchester, A.D. 1586–1602. By JOHN
HARLAND, Esq. *pp.* viii, 128.

Twenty-third year (1865–6).

LXVI. The Stanley Papers. Part III. Private Devotions and Miscellanies of James seventh earl of
Derby, K.G., with a prefatory Memoir and Appendix of Documents. Edited by the Rev. CANON
RAINES, M.A., F.S.A. Vol. I. *pp.* i-ccviii. *Four Plates.*
LXVII. The Stanley Papers. Part III. Vol. II. *pp.* ccix-cccxcv. *Four Plates.*
LXVIII. Collectanea relating to Manchester and its Neighbourhood, at various periods. Compiled,
arranged and edited by JOHN HARLAND, F.S.A. Vol. I. *pp.* viii, 258.

Twenty-fourth year (1866–7).

LXIX. The Admission Register of the Manchester School, with some Notices of the more distinguished
Scholars. Edited by the Rev. JEREMIAH FINCH SMITH, M.A., Rector of Aldridge, Staffordshire,
and Rural Dean. Vol. I., from A.D. 1730 to A.D. 1775. *pp.* viii, 253.
LXX. The Stanley Papers. Part III. Vol. 3. *(Conclusion.)* *pp.* 112 and 65. *Frontispiece.*
LXXI. Collectanea Anglo-Poetica. Part III. *pp.* x, 282.

Twenty-fifth year (1867-8).

LXXII. Collectanea relating to Manchester and its neighbourhood. Vol. II. *pp.* viii. 252.
LXXIII. The Admission Register of the Manchester School, with some Notices of the more dis-
tinguished Scholars. Vol. II., from A.D. 1775 to April A.D. 1807. *pp.* v, 302.
LXXIV. Three Lancashire Documents of the Fourteenth and Fifteenth Centuries, namely : I. The
Great De Lacy Inquisition, Feb. 16, 1311. II. Survey of 1320–1346. III. Custom Roll and Rental
of the manor of Ashton-under-Lyne. 1421. Edited by JOHN HARLAND, Esq., F.S.A. *pp.* xiii, 140.

Twenty sixth year (1868-9).

VOL.

LXXV. Lancashire Funerals Certificates. Edited by THOMAS WILLIAM KING, Esq., F.S.A., York Herald. With additions by the Rev. F. R. RAINES, M.A., F.S.A., Vice President of the Chetham Society. *pp.* viii, 102.

LXXVI. Observations and Instructions divine and morall. In Verse. By Robert Heywood of Heywood, Lancashire. Edited by JAMES CROSSLEY, Esq., F.S.A. *pp.* xxiv, 108.

LXXVII. Collectanea Anglo-Poetica. Part IV. *pp.* vi, 283-542.

Twenty-seventh year (1869-70).

LXXVIII. Tracts written in the Controversy respecting the Legitimacy of Amicia, daughter of Hugh Cyveliok, earl of Chester. A.D. 1673-1679. By sir Peter Leycester, bart., and sir Thomas Mainwaring, bart. Reprinted from the Collection at Peover. Edited, with an Introduction, by WILLIAM BEAMONT, Esq. Part I. *pp.* xcv, 94. *Portrait of sir Peter Leycester.*

LXXIX. Tracts written in the Controversy respecting the Legitimacy of Amicia. Part II. *pp.* 95-322. *Portrait of sir Thomas Mainwaring.*

LXXX. Tracts written in the Controversy respecting the Legitimacy of Amicia. Part III. (*Conclusion.*) *pp.* 323-550. *With frontispiece of Stall at Peover.*

Twenty-eighth year (1870-1).

LXXXI. The Visitation of the County Palatine of Lancaster, made in the year 1567, by William Flower, Esq., Norroy king of arms. Edited by the Rev. F. R. RAINES, M.A., F.S.A., Vicar of Milnrow, and Hon. Canon of Manchester. *pp.* xvi, 141.

LXXXII. The Visitation of the County Palatine of Lancaster, made in the year 1613, by Richard St. George, Esq., Norroy king of arms. Edited by the Rev. F. R. RAINES, M.A., F.S.A., Vicar of Milnrow, Hon. Canon of Manchester, and Rural Dean. *pp.* xx, 142.

LXXXIII. Chetham Miscellanies, Vol. IV., containing:

Some Account of General Robert Venables, of Antrobus and Wincham, Cheshire ; with an engraving from his Portrait at Wincham, together with the Autobiographical Memoranda or Diary of his Widow, Elizabeth Venables. From the original MS. in the possession of LEE P. TOWNSHEND, Esq. *pp* iv, 28. *Pedigree* 1. *Portrait of General Robert Venables.*

A Forme of Confession grounded vpon the Ancient Catholique and Apostolique Faith. Made and composed by the honorable ladie The Lady Bridget Egerton. A.D. 1636. From the original MS. in the possession of SIR PHILIP DE MALPAS GREY EGERTON, Bart., M.P. *pp.* vi, 23. *Pedigrees* 2. *Plate.*

A Kalender conteyning the Names of all such Gent. and others as upon her Maty's Pryvye Seales have paid there Money to the handes of Sir Hugh Cholmondley Knyghte Collect' of Her Hyghnes Loane with[in] the Countie of Chester, together wth the severall Somes and Daies of Receipt. A.D. 1597. From the original MS. in the possession of R. H. WOOD, Esq., F.S.A. *pp.* iv, 4.

History of Warrington Friary. Edited by WILLIAM BEAMONT, Esq. *pp.* vii, 76. *Index* 4. *Four Plates, being Effigies and Arms, Tombstones, and Fragments.*

Twenty-ninth year (1871-2).

LXXXIV. The Visitation of the County Palatine of Lancaster, made in the year 1664-5, by Sir William Dugdale, Knight, Norroy king of arms. Edited by the Rev. F. R. RAINES, M.A., F.S.A., Vicar of Milnrow, Hon. Canon of Manchester, and Rural Dean. Part I. *pp.* xiv, 104.

LXXXV. The Visitation of the County Palatine of Lancaster, made in the year 1664-5, by Sir William Dugdale, Knight. Part II. *pp.* 105-224.

LXXXVI. Annals of the Lords of Warrington for the first five centuries after the conquest. With historical notices of the place and neighbourhood. Edited by WILLIAM BEAMONT, Esq. Part I. *pp.* xxvi, 262. *Three Plates.*

Thirtieth year (1872-3).

LXXXVII. Annals of the Lords of Warrington for the first five centuries after the conquest. Part II. (*Conclusion.*) *pp.* 263-523. *Index* 11. *Three Plates.*

LXXXVIII. The Visitation of the County Palatine of Lancaster, made in the year 1664-5, by Sir William Dugdale, Knight. Part III. (*Conclusion.*) *pp.* 225-344. *Index* 17.

LXXXIX. The Dr. Farmer Chetham MS., being a commonplace-book in the Chetham Library, temp. Elizabeth, James I. and Charles I., consisting of verse and prose, mostly hitherto unpublished. Edited, with Introduction and Notes, by the Rev. ALEXANDER B. GROSART. Part I. *pp.* xvi, 120. *Frontispiece in Photo-lithography.*

REMAINS

HISTORICAL & LITERARY

CONNECTED WITH THE PALATINE COUNTIES OF

LANCASTER AND CHESTER.

PUBLISHED BY

THE CHETHAM SOCIETY.

VOL. CIX.

PRINTED FOR THE CHETHAM SOCIETY.
M.DCCC.LXXX.

COUNCIL for 1879–80.

THE

CORRESPONDENCE

OF

𝕹𝖆𝖙𝖍𝖆𝖓 𝖂𝖆𝖑𝖜𝖔𝖗𝖙𝖍 𝖆𝖓𝖉 𝕻𝖊𝖙𝖊𝖗 𝕾𝖊𝖉𝖉𝖔𝖓

OF OUTWOOD,

AND

OTHER DOCUMENTS CHIEFLY RELATING TO THE
BUILDING OF RINGLEY CHAPEL.

EDITED, WITH NOTES, BY
JOHN SAMUEL FLETCHER.

"I would some wyse man had the perusall of our letters."
NATHAN WALWORTH.

PRINTED FOR THE CHETHAM SOCIETY.
M.DCCC.LXXX.

PRINTED BY CHARLES E. SIMMS
MANCHESTER.

PREFACE.

THE Correspondence of Nathan Walworth, preserved among the deeds relating to Ringley Chapel for more than 200 years, was shown to the late Bishop of Manchester, who expressed a strong opinion that it ought to be published.

The Editorship was undertaken by the late ROBERT SCARR SOWLER, Esq., Q.C., a gentleman well qualified by his literary tastes, and the interest he took in Ringley, where, as senior warden, he laid the foundation stone of the present church in 1850.

Mr. Sowler made a few memoranda upon the letters, which I have distinguished by the initials R. S. S., but at his death in 1873 he had not made any further progress, and the preparation of the letters was suspended till the Council of the Chetham Society entrusted them to me.

In finishing my task, which has been a very pleasant one, I wish to thank the Rev. S. BARTLET, late incumbent of Ringley, and the TRUSTEES of the church, for their courtesy in giving me every information in their power.

I wish also to acknowledge my obligations to J. E. BAILEY, Esq., F.S.A., a gentleman who has made a special study of Presbyterian government in Lancashire under the Commonwealth ; and to the late Canon RAINES of Milnrow, whose *MS.* collections and great personal knowledge of genealogy, always most kindly communicated, were invaluable to the student of local history.

I am also indebted to the "Local Gleanings" of the *Manchester Courier* for much interesting information (see especially Nos. 59 and 67).

I cannot conclude more fitly than in the words of the late Canon Parkinson : "Should it be deemed by the learned reader that the notes upon some topics are copious to redundancy, he is requested to bear in mind that the Chetham Society is not comprised simply of scholars and antiquarians, but of persons who take a natural and deep interest in everything which illustrates the history of the two Palatine counties.

" It was, therefore, the object of the Editor to produce for such readers a book which might be read by itself, and without constant reference to such works as are not always at hand to the general reader" (see Preface to the *Life of Adam Martindale*).

INTRODUCTION.

Of Nathan Walworth; of Peter Seddon; of Baynard's Castle; of the Earls of Pembroke; of Bishop Bridgeman; of Ringley Chapel and its incumbents.

NATHAN WALWORTH or Wallwork, as the name was originally spelled, was the son of Ellis Walworth of Ringley-fold in the Outwood of Pilkington, where he was born in the year 1572.

Nathan's family had long been settled at Ringley. I learn from Canon Raines that as early as 1420, in a settlement of the estate of Sir John de Pilkington, William Walwerk is mentioned as the occupier of "one pasture called Ryngleys." In the Will of Laurence Walwork of Prestwich, proved in 1563, Ellis Walwork (probably Nathan's father) is appointed "supervisor," and it is interesting to note a bequest of 6s. 8d. towards the repair of Prestwich church.

Nathan tells us that, though born in Lancashire, he was "bred" in Wiltshire, very likely in the house of his relative Ralph Walwork, who had property in Salisbury. He was not educated at either university, for he "occupied places of trust" from the age of seventeen (see letter 35). From an expression in another letter, it seems probable that Nathan was intended for the law, but ultimately he

entered the service of the Herbert family, and became
steward to William, third Earl of Pembroke, and to
Philip, who succeeded his brother as fourth earl in 1630.
Of these two noblemen Nathan says nothing in his
letters.   Little that was creditable could be said about
Earl Philip, and the old steward, who had known him as
"worthy young Sir Philip," a handsome, well-dressed
youth, was perhaps blind to the eccentricities of his
master, and prefers to grumble after his fashion at his
mistress, the celebrated Countess Anne.   "O that you
served the mistress I serve," he writes, when rebuking
Peter Seddon for his shortcomings, and in another letter
he complains very quaintly of his want of leisure when
the countess was at home.   Yet I think Nathan must have
been attached to so excellent a woman as Anne, while
she must have found the faithful steward an invaluable
friend when left alone by her reckless husband in a huge
mansion like Baynard's Castle, which she describes in her
Memoir as "full of riches and more secured by my lying
there."

Throughout these letters Nathan assumes a certain
tone of superiority towards his friend, partly, I think,
because he was some years older than 'neighbour Peter,'
and partly because his position as steward to a great
nobleman, and his frequent journeys about England on
Lord Pembroke's business, made him more a man of the
world than Peter, who was content to live on and by his
paternal acres ; it is the difference between the town and
country mouse.   But though Nathan often scolds ' neigh-

bour Peter' for being over thrifty and dilatory in helping
on the school and chapel, yet he seems to have been
much attached to him; and it is remarkable, that in his
Will, which contains some ninety bequests, neither Peter
nor any of his family are mentioned.

In July 1640 Nathan was present at " Commemoration" at Oxford, and he writes : " I was mery amonge
the Doctors, in the midst of their Disputations, where I
was lyke to have my belly burst and my ribs broken in
the crowde, my shirt stucke to my backe, and sweat
trickled down my cheekes, and yet I could have endured
it to this day." He was probably in attendance on Lord
Pembroke, then high steward of the university.

In his last two letters, written in December 1640,
Nathan speaks of failing health, and he died very shortly
afterwards, perhaps of the plague, which, as the register
of St. Benet's shows, was very prevalent in Castle Baynard's Ward during the years 1640 and 1641.

Both Nathan and Peter were Puritans in theology and
modes of thought. It is observable, that in describing
his journey from Hull to London in August 1639, Nathan
records that he "rested Sonday" at Huntingdon; he
dedicated Ringley chapel to no saint, but to the " Holy
Saviour," and at the commencement of his Will he gives,
as was then the custom, an eloquent exposition of his
religious belief.

We know that the preaching of John Bradford and
Geo. Marsh in the neighbouring parish of Dean, and
their subsequent martyrdom, strongly influenced the

Lancashire people in favour of Puritanism. Oliver Heywood says of the adjoining district of Little Lever, "it hath long been famous for glorious professors and powerful preachers, and I take it as one of the great mercies of my life that my nativity was in Goshen, under the star of Jacob's special influence."

The letters, 57 in number, extend over a period of seventeen years, from June 1623 to December 1640. They seem to show that Nathan's life, though busy and prosperous, was not eventful; yet he lived in stirring times, and being in the service of two Court Chamberlains, and also the friend of Sir Thomas Lyster, physician to Queen Anne of Denmark, he must have heard all the court gossip, and it is a pity he was not more communicative about the politics of the day.

Nathan's nearest relatives were his younger brother Peter, who died in 1627, and his two nephews Ellis and Nathan. Ellis Walworth lived at Ringley Fold, where he entertained Mr. Angier on his first visit to Ringley in 1629, and where his widow provided a collation of "wine and banketing stuff" for Bishop Bridgeman, when he rode over from Lever to consecrate the chapel. Ellis died in 1630, and left his uncle overseer of his Will and guardian of his infant daughters, one of whom, Mary, afterwards married Nathan Morte of Deane. Nathan, often mentioned in the letters as "cousin Nathan," survived his uncle, who made him his residuary legatee. Nathan, the younger, lived at Old Hall in Pilkington. He married in 1647, Maria Pollit of Prestwich, and died in 1677,[1] leaving a son also called Nathan, who married Ellen Grundie at Prestwich in 1685.

Nathan Walworth's letters give me the idea of a shrewd old batchelor, with a pet "katt"; active and sociable in his habits and fond of a day's fishing or coursing in the intervals of business. Canon Raines applied to him Pisanio's description,[2] as one of "a waggish courage, ready in gibes, quick-answered, saucy, and as quarrellous as the weasel." It should be added that he was of a kindly nature, thoughtful for others, and generously anxious to share his prosperity with his kinsfolk and his native place.

Family of Nathan Walworth.

William Walwerk held land at Ringley, of Sir John Pilkington, in 1420.

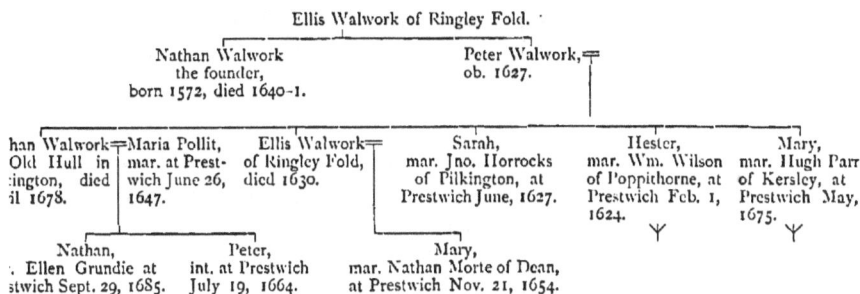

Ellis Walwork of Ringley Fold.

Nathan Walwork the founder, born 1572, died 1640-1.	Peter Walwork, ᵼ ob. 1627.

| han Walwork⹋Maria Pollit, Old Hull in mar. at Prest- :ington, died wich June 26, il 1678. 1647. | Ellis Walwork⹋ of Ringley Fold, died 1630. | Sarah, mar. Jno. Horrocks of Pilkington, at Prestwich June, 1627. | Hester, mar. Wm. Wilson of Poppithorne, at Prestwich Feb. 1, 1624. ᵼ | Mary, mar. Hugh Parr of Kersley, at Prestwich May, 1675. ᵼ |

| Nathan, ⁚. Ellen Grundie at stwich Sept. 29, 1685. | Peter, int. at Prestwich July 19, 1664. | Mary, mar. Nathan Morte of Dean, at Prestwich Nov. 21, 1654. |

[1] See the *Manchester Court Leet Record* where he is called " Captain Nathan Walworth."

[2] *Cymbeline,* act iii, sc. 4.

PETER SEDDON of Prestolee, in the Outwood of Pilkington, to whom Walworth's letters are addressed, was the representative of a substantial yeoman family, who have lived on the banks of the Irwell for at least 400 years.

The name was sometimes spelled Seddowne, Sedon or Sedan (as by Richard Sedan bailiff of Liverpool in 1683), and there is a tradition that the first family, or families, so called, came from Sedan on the Meuse, and took their surname from that town.

This is not improbable, as Sedan has long been famous for its manufacture of woollen goods, and we know that about the year 1337 Flemish clothiers, encouraged by the wise policy of Edward III.,[3] settled in Rochdale and Bolton, where they introduced wooden clogs and "jannock," or oat-meal loaves. However derived, the name of Seddon, rarely found elsewhere, has always flourished in the neighbourhood of Bolton. In 1513 John Seddon accompanied Sir Richard Assheton of Middleton to the battle-field of Flodden, and his name and effigy, the first of a row of seventeen, is preserved in a painted window in Middleton church.[4] In a subsidy roll for the Hundred of Salford, dated 8 March, 15 Henry VIII. (1524), Richard Seddon of Bury parish is mentioned as paying a tax of 40s. An earlier Richard Seddon,[5] connected, through his wife Joan, with the families of Standish and Radford, held land worth five marks yearly at Kyrsley,

---

[3] 2 Edward III., c. 1.

[4] Mr. Corser's notes to *Iter Lancastrense*, pp. 38—40, and front.

[5] Rental of Thomas West, *Harl. MSS.*, cod. 2112, fol. 166.

in Farnworth, of Thomas West, "lord of Mamcestre" (1 May 1473), and from this worthy Peter Seddon was seventh in descent, according to a pedigree copied by Mr. Barritt in 1789,[f] and confirmed by the *Manchester Court Leet Records*, and some entries in the *Calendar to Pleadings of the Duchy of Lancaster.*

Neighbour Peter was the eldest son of Raphe Seddon of Prestolee, and Mary, eldest daughter of William Foxe of the Rhodes, in Pilkington, "clerk comptroller" of the household of Henry earl of Derby.

Peter Seddon had five younger brothers, John, Henry, William, Thomas and George. Of these, Henry was probably the Henry Seddon, who served as elder of Deane in the "classis" that met at Bury in 1647; William was educated at Magdalen College, Cambridge, and took holy orders. He was the first person that preached at Ringley chapel, and he remained there from 1626 to 1629. During the Civil War he was an ardent Royalist, and suffered for his opinions. He applied for help to Peter, who replied that "would he conform himselfe to ye Godly party his own merits would protect and prefer him."

Neighbour Peter himself was an active supporter of Presbyterian government under the Commonwealth, notwithstanding the influence of his mother's relatives, who were Royalists.

In 164½, Peter and his brother Thomas, and his sons

[f] *Barritt MSS.*, in the Chetham Library.

Peter, Raphe and Robert, "took the Protestation " or oath
to defend the Protestant church, his majesty's person and
power, the privilege of parliament and the lawful rights
and liberties of the people. In 1646 he attended the
"classis" at Preston with Henry Seddon, and subsequently he served with John Walworth as elder of
Ringley in the Manchester classis, and the minute book
shows that he attended the meetings regularly, though he
was not present on the occasion when his youngest son
Robert,[7] then minister at Gorton, was examined before
the classis in "Hebrew, Greek, Logic, Philosophy, Ethics,
Physics and Metaphysics," and approved (May 1654).

The same year (19 May), Peter Seddon acted, with
Ralph Smith of Unswood, as a commissioner, under an
act of Parliament, for reconveying certain lands at Chetham, forfeited for treason, to Edward Chetham, on payment of a fine.

" Neighbour" Peter survived the Restoration, and in
his will, dated July 1662, mentions that he is in good
health, though over eighty, and thanks God, "who has
lengthened the threads of my life more than any of my
ancestors." Amongst other bequests he leaves his eldest
son Peter all his books, and "the wainscott and seelinge
along the walls and sides of this house." He died the
following year, aged 84, and was buried in .Ringley
churchyard, where his tombstone yet exists, and his
descendants still bury their dead.

---

[7] Erroneously called *Ralph* in Dr. Halley's *Lancashire, its Puritanism,*
&c., vol. i, p. 450.

Peter Seddon was married, at Prestwich (December 1612), to his cousin Ellen Seddon, by whom he had four sons and three daughters. Of these sons, Peter, the eldest, became a zealous Presbyterian. He served as a captain in the Parliament army, and took part in the rising, under Sir Geo. Booth, in 1569; and in 1672 his house at Prestolee was licensed as a meeting house. John, the third son, was a captain in the Royal army in Cumberland[8] when the civil war began, but I know nothing of his subsequent career. Robert, Peter's youngest son, already alluded to, was a strong Presbyterian like his father and eldest brother, and became a noted preacher. Ejected from his vicarage of Langley in 1662, he finally settled at Bolton, where he gave the site for a Presbyterian chapel, which was opened the year after his death. Robert Seddon died in 1695, while on a visit to his brother Peter, in the house in which he was born, and he was buried in his father's grave.[9]

Among 'neighbour' Peter's kinsfolk were Dr. Laurence Seddon, prebendary of Hereford, and rector of Worthen in Shropshire (where he died in September 1675); and John Seddon, a noted professor of caligraphy, and author of *The Penman's Paradise*, who died in 1700, aged 55.[10] I may also mention the Rev. Thomas Seddon, curate of Stretford, and incumbent of Lydgate in Saddleworth in 1789. He was the author of several works, and in

[8] See No. 58 and note.
[9] See also note to letter 50.
[10] Noble's *Continuation of Grainger's Biograph. Hist.*, vol. i, p. 311.

his "letters written to an officer in the army"[11] (viz., his brother, General Daniel Seddon), he says : " It is in my power to trace my pedigree up to the Conquest, for with the Conqueror my ancestors first came into this country, as appears from the testimony of grants for services done in that successful enterprise, which are now in the possession of a distant relative, a gentleman of my own name." It is not a little amusing that the writer should think it necessary to give this information to his own brother !

Another descendant of Peter Seddon's was Thomas Seddon the painter, who died at Cairo, 23 November 1856, aged 35. His picture " Jerusalem" was purchased by subscription after his death for 600*l*. and presented to the National Gallery.

By the custom of the manors of Pilkington and Darcy Lever, leases were granted for successive lives, and, on the determination of the last, were renewed to the eldest son of the tenant for three lives, at a proportionate fine. In this manner the Seddons lived at Prestolee as tenants of the earls of Derby for at least nine generations, till the death of James Seddon in 1846.

Dr. Franklin boasts that his ancestors "lived in the same village (Ecton in Northamptonshire), on a freehold of about 30 acres, for at least 300 years," and Mr. Hayward tells us[12] that the Webber family "have occupied the Halberton Court farm (near Tiverton) as renting farmers for more than 200 years," but the case of a family

---

[11] Printed by Eyre's of Warrington in 1786, and now very rare.
[12] Hayward's *Essays*, 3rd series, p. 290.

holding the same land of the same landlords for over 300 years is perhaps unique.   (See family tree at end of vol.)

B-aynard's Castle, where Nathan Walworth dates his letters, and where he lived as Lord Pembroke's steward, stood on the north bank of the Thames, below St. Paul's Cathedral, on the site now occupied by Castle Baynard's wharf, in Upper Thames street.

Stow, in his *Survey of London*, tells us "it was so called of Baynard, a nobleman that came in with the Conqueror," probably identical with Bainardus, mentioned in *Domesday* as the most considerable tenant of the Abbot of Westminster.

It is said that Baynard gave his name to Bayswater, which is described in a deed as late as 1653 as Baynard's Watering Place.[13]

The Castle was forfeited by the descendants of the founder, and granted to one of the sons of Gilbert de Clare, earl of Pembroke, in whose family it remained for three centuries.

Humphrey, duke of Gloucester and earl of Pembroke, rebuilt the castle in 1628, after it had been almost destroyed by fire, and after his attainder it was assigned to Richard duke of York, who "lodged there as in his own house."

When his son, Edward earl of March, entered London

[13] *Notes and Queries*, 1 ser., vol. i, p. 162.

after the battle of Mortimer's Cross, he took up his residence at Baynard's Castle, for we read that on Sunday, 2 March 1461, the throne was offered to him, "then being lodged at his castle of Baynard," by the earl of Warwick and others, and he was proclaimed at Westminster the next day as Edward IV. His brother Richard also lived at the castle, and Sir Thomas More also records that on 24 June 1483, the duke of Buckingham, the lord mayor of London, and many others, went to Richard at Baynard's Castle, and there solicited him to become their king.[14]

In 1501, Henry VII., who, it may be noted, was the nephew and representative of Jasper Tudor, Earl of Pembroke, "repaired or rather new-built this house not embattled, or so strongly fortified castle-like, but far more beautiful and commodious for the entertainment of any prince," and the king seems to have lodged there frequently.

In February 1536, shortly after the death of Queen Katherine of Arragon, a copious inventory was taken of "alle and singuler Warderobe Stuffe remayning within Baynardes Castille whiche late was the Princesse Dowgiers," and about the same time Henry VIII. granted Baynard's Castle to the Duke of Richmond, his natural son by Eliz. Blount, who died himself the following July.[15]

The castle was perhaps considered as a kind of

---

[14] Shakespeare's *Richard III.*, act iii, sc. 7.

[15] *Camden Miscellany*, vol. iii.

appanage to the Earldom of Pembroke, for we read that in February 1553, William Herbert, created Earl of Pembroke two years before, "rode to his mansion of Baynard's Castle with a retinue of 300 horsemen, of whom 100 were gentlemen in plain blue cloth, with chains of gold and badges of a dragon on their sleeves."

Five months later the Council, after consulting with the lord mayor and the earls of Shrewsbury and Pembroke at Baynard's Castle, decided to proclaim Queen Mary.

In 1603 the castle still belonged to the earls of Pembroke, who were probably tenants at will under the Crown, and on 1 July 1641 (about six months after Nathan Walworth's death), Philip, the fourth earl, was here installed chancellor of the University of Oxford, and here lived Anne, his second countess, while her husband resided at the Cock-pit at White-hall.

Pepys tells us that on 19 June 1660, just three weeks after his Restoration, Charles II. went with Lord Sandwich to sup at Baynard's Castle. A few years later the castle perished in the Great Fire, but it still gives its name to the ward of Castle Baynard.

The view of the castle (see end of letters) has been photographed, by the kind permission of J. G. Crace, Esq., from an engraving in his collection of maps and views of London, now in the Kensington Museum. It represents the castle as it appeared in 1649, about eight years after Nathan Walworth's death.

WILLIAM HERBERT, in whose household Nathan Walworth served as steward, was born in 1580, and succeeded his father as third earl of Pembroke in 1601. His mother was Mary, sister of the famous Sir Philip Sidney, who dedicated to her his *Arcadia*.

The earl inherited his mother's beauty. He is described as "the very picture and viva effigies of nobilitas, a person truly generous, a singular lover of learning and the professors thereof," and there is strong reason for thinking that he was the beloved friend to whom Shakespeare addressed many of his sonnets. He married Mary, eldest daughter of George earl of Shrewsbury, and died without surviving issue in April 1630. Like his younger brother after him, William Herbert was made lord-chamberlain and chancellor of the University of Oxford (1626). He presented the University with a large collection of *MSS.*, and Pembroke College (formerly Broadgates Hall) was named after him, but he is best remembered as the "Pembroke" mentioned in Ben Jonson's epitaph on his mother:

> "Vnderneath this marble hearse
> Lies the subject of all verse
> Sidney's sister, Pembroke's mother," &c.

PHILIP HERBERT, also the nephew and probably the godson of Sir Philip Sidney, succeeded his brother as fourth earl of Pembroke, having been already raised to the peerage as Baron Shurland and Earl of Montgomery. He married, first, Susan, daughter of Edward Vere, earl of

Oxford, and sister of Elizabeth, the wife of William, earl of Derby; and secondly (3 June 1630), Anne Clifford, whose aunt Margaret was the wife of Henry, fourth earl of Derby. Earl Philip was thus connected with the Stanleys through both his wives. The earl had a handsome person and dressed with care, which obtained him the favour of king James, of whom a contemporary writes, "the king is nicely heedful of such points and dwelleth on good looks and handsome accoutrements."

Lord Pembroke was made chamberlain to Charles I., and broke his official staff over the shoulders of Thomas May, the historian, at a masque at Whitehall. Subsequently he was deprived of his office for "raising a brawl" in the House of Lords, and in revenge for this disgrace he supported the popular cause with his wealth and influence. On the attainder of Archbishop Laud, he was made chancellor of Oxford, and he sat in the Rump Parliament, as member for Berkshire, shortly before his death in 1650.

Wood (*Fasti*, i, 314) describes the earl as "a very frequent swearer and one intolerably choleric, quarrelsome and offensive." A bitter satire on him, attributed to Samuel Butler, and purporting to be "the last Will and Testament of Philip, earl of Pembroke," is quoted by Hartley Coleridge (cf. *Worthies of Yorkshire*, pp. 282-4). The earl was anything but a good husband. We find his second wife writing thus of him in 1638: "I dare not venture to come up [to town] without his leave, lest he should take that occasion to turn me out of his house, as he did out of Whitehall, and then I shall not know where to put my head."[16]

ANNE CLIFFORD, whose complaint has just been quoted, was the daughter and heiress of George, third earl of Cumberland, and widow of Richard, earl of Dorset. In her *Memoirs* the countess thus describes herself: " The colour of mine eyes was black like my father's and the aspect of them was quick and lively like my mother's. My hair was brown and very thick and so long that it reached to the calf of my leg, when I stood upright, with a peak of hair on my forehead and a dimple on my chin and an exquisite shape of body like my father's. And, though I say it, the perfections of my mind were much above those of my body. I had a strong and copious memory, a sound judgement and a discerning spirit." By her tutor, Samuel Daniel, the friend of Spenser and Ben Jonson, Anne was carefully educated and " nurtured in the precepts and practice of economy, self-denial, domestic order and

> " Pure religion teaching household laws."

And she afterwards showed her gratitude for Daniel's instruction by erecting a monument to his memory. In spite of her wealth, virtues, great abilities, and a fair share of good looks, Anne Clifford was not happy with either of her husbands, of whom the first was a profligate and a spendthrift, and the second so violent and eccentric as to

[16] See Whitaker's *Hist. of Craven.*

be at times hardly sane. As she quaintly puts it, " I lived in both these my Lords' great families, as the river Rhodanus runs through the lake of Geneva, without mingling any part of its stream with that lake." Perhaps the fault was not entirely on the side of the husband if we allow weight to Dr. Whittaker's opinion that "Anne's features were more expressive of firmness than benignity." However this may be, it was not till after Lord Pembroke's death that the countess had full scope for her energy and benevolence.

During her second widowhood Anne resided almost wholly on the northern estates, occupied in repairing the damages of war and neglect and in deeds of charity. She protected the distressed royalists, particularly the learned and the clergy, and as a symbol of the ancient loyalty of her race she planted at Skipton an acorn from the oak of Boscobel, which grew up to be a noble tree, and "long survived the fortunes of that regal family, whose deliverance it commemorated."

Besides restoring her six castles of Brough, Brougham, Pendragon, Appleby, Barden and Skipton, and erecting magnificent monuments to her father at Skipton and her mother at Appleby, the countess repaired seven churches and founded two hospitals, "works of which she took care not to lose the credit with posterity," remarks Hartly Coleridge; and he adds, "as long as stone or marble can perpetuate the memory of the just, hers will continue in Westmoreland and Craven.

Dr. Donne said of Anne, that "she knew well how to

discourse of all things from predestination down to slea silk," and Whitaker eloquently sums up his account of her by saying, " she diffused plenty and happiness around her by consuming the produce of her vast domains in hospitality and charity. Equally remote from the un-distinguishing profusion of ancient times and the parsi-monious elegance of modern manners, her house was a school for the young, a retreat for the aged, an asylum for the persecuted, a college for the learned and a pattern for all." Anne died March 1675, in her eighty-seventh year, and was buried by the side of her mother at Ap-pleby.[17]

JOHN BRIDGEMAN, bishop of Chester, often alluded to as " ye B.B." in Walworth's letters, was the son of Edward Bridgeman of Exeter, Esq., sheriff of Devon in 1578. He was educated at Cambridge, where he became Fellow and afterwards Master of Magdalene College. He was also domestic chaplain to James I., who gave him the rectory of Wigan in 1615. He was then made preben-dary of Lichfield and Peterborough, and finally conse-crated bishop of Chester in 1619, and in addition he appears to have held the living of Bangor.

About the year 1629 he purchased the manor of Great Lever from Sir Ralph Assheton, whose father bought the estate from a descendant of the Radfords. Four years later (1633) the bishop was required by the king's council

[17] See Hartley Coleridge's *Worthies of Yorkshire*, and Whitaker's *History of Craven.*

to investigate the case of seventeen witches from Pendle, condemned to death at the Lancaster assizes, and the inquiry resulted in their acquittal. In 1637 the bishop presented to the cathedral a large and richly-carved pulpit of wood, which is still preserved. The same year Prynne passed through Chester on his way to be imprisoned in Carnarvon castle. His ears had been cut off, and his cheeks branded with the letters "S. L." as a seditious libeller, and in this condition he travelled twenty-five days on horse-back. Two tradesmen of Chester, named Ince, and John Bruen of Stapleford, near Tarvin (the son of an eminent Puritan of the same name), openly sympathised with Prynne on this occasion, but Bishop Bridgeman compelled them to make a public acknowledgment of their fault in the cathedral. When the Parliament troops surounded Chester in 1645, "the aged bishop dreading the hardships of a siege voided the place"; he had already been fined 3,000l. by the Parliament, and in 1650 his palace, with all the furniture, was sold for 1059l. The bishop retired to Moreton in Shropshire, and died there, in poverty, in 1658. He was buried in Kinnersley church, where his great-grandson, Sir John Bridgeman, erected a monument to his memory in 1719.

Bishop Bridgeman married Eliza, daughter of Dr. Helyar, canon of Exeter, by whom he had five sons. Of these, Henry, the third, married Katharine, daughter of Robert Lever of Lever, and became bishop of Man; the eldest son, Orlando, was the lineal ancestor of the

present earl of Bradford, who still owns the estate at
Great Lever.

RINGLEY CHAPEL appears to have been the first built
and endowed in Lancashire by private benevolence after
the Reformation.

The view of Ringley (see p. 1) has been engraved
for this work from an oil painting, executed in the last
century, and now in possession of Isaac Whittaker, Esq.,
one of the trustees of the present church. This view is
taken from the Kersley bank of the river Irwell, near the
present vicarage, and gives, I believe, the only repre-
sentation of the old chapel still existing. The building
on the right stands on, or near, the site of Ringley Fold,
where Nathan was born. The old chapel contained the
following inscription, still preserved in the present
building :

"This Chappell was erected at yᵉ cost and charges of Nathan Walworthe some to Ellis Walworthe Anº Do 1625, Anº que ætatis suæ 54
            'En dedi vobis exempl pergite' John 13. 15
                'Vade et tu fac similiter' Luc. 10. 37
                'Euge serue bone et fidelis' Matt. 25. 21.
            'Ex tuo tibi dedi Domini non meo' 1 Chron. 29."

The chapel was licensed in February 1627, and Whittle[13]
tells us that William Seddon was the first preacher, and
that he remained there till 1629. In the summer of that
year John Angier was ordained and preached his first
sermon at Ringley, and many followed him (says Oliver

            [13] *History of Bolton*, p. 36.

Heywood) to Ellis Walworth's house in Ringley Fold, and desired him to be their minister.

Mr. Angier preached for some months and then, being suspended by Bishop Bridgeman, removed to Denton. In referring to this Mr. Angier thanks God, "who carried the work of my ministry through inhibition, suspensions, excommunications, in time of the height of the power and persecution of the bishops; though I might not runne the race of one year at Ringley-chappel, whither I was first called, and in that imperfect year was twice inhibited."[19]

The chapel was not consecrated by Bishop Bridgeman until December 1634. On this occasion Nathan was unable to be present, and 'neighbour' Peter wrote him a long and graphic account of the ceremony, which has fortunately been preserved.

The following year William Hulton, one of the Hultons of Farnworth,[20] was appointed minister on Nathan's recommendation. Mr. Hulton was probably ejected in 1647, when Thomas Holland became minister, having "received a call" to Ringley, where he officiated till 1653.

Amongst other incumbents of Ringley I may mention John Angier, junior, the son of John Angier of Denton, who was appointed in 1657; Joshua Dixon (1691), who preached the funeral sermon of William Hulme, the founder of the Hulmeian exhibitions; Jacob Scholes

---

[19] See *An Helpe to better Hearts for better times*, by John Angier. Pastor of Denton. London 1647. From a copy in the possession of Mr. Bailey.

[20] See No. 27 and note.

d

(1719), who in 1721 procured a faculty enabling him to erect a gallery in the chapel and to let the pews "at reasonable rates for his own profit and that of his successors," and James Brennan (1767), who died in the pulpit whilst preaching, 3 September 1787.

Amongst the benefactors of Ringley was William Assheton, rector of Prestwich (1685–1731), whose long Latin epitaph there commences with the quaint prayer, " Deus te amet qui hæc legis " (God bless the reader of this epitaph).

Mr. Assheton gave 200*l*. in 1709 towards the endowment of the chapel, to meet a like grant from the governors of Queen Anne's bounty, and the money was invested in land near Bury and now produces 36*l*. a year.

In 1846 James Seddon, the last of his family who lived at Prestolee, having previously built a new school-house, bequeathed 1000*l*. towards the school endowment, and the scholars, out of gratitude, used to come and sing under the windows of his house in Whit-week, and continued the custom for fifteen years after his death.

In the year 1827 Ringley chapel was entirely rebuilt, from the designs of the late Sir Charles Barry, then a very young man. This chapel, being found too small, was pulled down in 1850, and the foundation stone of the present building was laid by R. S. Sowler, Esq., Q. C., as senior churchwarden.

The picturesque tower by Barry remains standing by itself in the churchyard, and contains a stone from the original chapel with the inscription.

> "In 1625
> Nathan Walworth builded me."

The portrait of Nathan has been engraved for the frontispiece of this work, from the original oil-painting preserved in the vestry of Ringley church. It represents him in his steward's dress, in his "closet" at Baynard's Castle, spectacles in hand, his account books around him and his keys of office, and "large chess-board black and white" hanging on the wainscot behind him.

Nathan's crest (viz., two arms, embowed, vested, gules, out of a ducal coronet, or, in hands proper a cake of bread argent), the same as that used by the famous Sir William Walworth, lord mayor of London, is blazoned on one of the chapel windows.

With Nathan Walworth's letters are printed three others; one written to him by Peter Seddon in 1634, in which the consecration of Ringley chapel is described at length; another written at the outbreak of the Civil War by Captain Peter Seddon to his brother John (then serving with the royal troops in Cumberland) with a postscript by "neighbour" Peter, and a third, lately printed in *Local Gleanings*, from the original in the Bodleian library, which gives an interesting account of William Seddon, written by his son Edward, the vicar of Throwley, in Devonshire.

I have added an abstract of Nathan's Will, and several other documents, which throw light on the persons and events alluded to in the letters.

J. S. F.

CONTENTS.

ILLUSTRATIONS.

CORRESPONDENCE OF NATHAN WALWORTH AND PETER SEDDON.

I. — *Addressed To my very kynd and loving Neighbour Peter Seddon in the Owtwoode, Pilkington.*

NEIGHBOUR Peter, I lyke and Accept of your lr̄es so well, that they shall not goe unanswered though (to use your fathers[1] owne wordes) I wryte but of the feightinge of Doggs in the Streets; I should thinke my self happy if I could but quyte[2] you w^t as good a Tale as you tolde me of my old fellow (or mayster) Ellis,[3] that durst not open his mouthe and Crye for feare least the stirke[4] should put hir horne into his mouth, and marr his Drinkinge, I doe not thinke but that boy will be a Councello^r before he Dye, seeing he is so pruydent, beinge so yonge,

for your Complementinge, of bringinge me on the way, it is better as it is, for it greevs me more to part from my frends, when we part in the way, then when I leave them at home, I can wryte no newes but what this bearer can tell you, therefore he shall save me that labour, and I will wryte no newes till I have as good a Tale, as that of ye boy and the stirke, and So w^t comendations to your self, and your wyfe your father and mother in law, I com̄it you to god and rest

Assuredlye Yours

Bay Castle   NATHAN WALWORTHE.

     June, 26. 1623.

[1] *yr. father.* Raphe Seddon, who died in 1612. But Nathan probably means Peter's father-in-law, William Seddon, who lived near him. (See No. 7 and note.)

[2] *quyte, i.e.,* quit; requite; repay. Cf. Milton. "One step higher would set me highest, and in a moment *quit* the debt immense of endless gratitude." *Par. Lost,* bk. iv, l. 51.

[3] *Ellis.* Perhaps Nathan's nephew, the son of Peter Walworth; but Ellis is a common Christian name in the neighbourhood.

[4] *stirke.* A yearling ox or heifer. Nathan is punning on the *horn* drinking cups then in use.

II.— *Addressed To my very lovinge frend Peter Seddon in the Owtwood.*

Neighbour Peter, I have longe expected your lr̄e to heare of your Agreement about this matter and am glad it is Comne so farr, I hope you will not lett it rest so, I for my part am readye to performe my promisse, either for Scoole or Chappell, if you resolve for a Chappell you must get my Lo:[5] consent, and Mr Langleyes,[6] and you must about agayne for greeter Alowance for if you can but reach to 80, 90, or 100*l.* that will be little Inough 'for a scoolemaister and you may fynd somethinge or other to lay it out on, wch will be worth 10*l.* per ann̄, wch a Scoolemayster will be content wt, with some small helps that will fall out, but where will you gett meanes for a Chaplayne ; for ye place, I lyke it well, and farr better then upō the other syde[7] of the water, and I lyke that by James Ouldam's[8] Barne better then the other and I thinke Mr Murrey[9] may be Compounded withall for little or nothinge, he is now with you, you may talke with him, as also about some trees, and then you may goe forward wt it this Springe, wch I Desyre and will pray yt god will lend me lyfe to see it performed, you may Conferr wt my brother[10] to whom I have also written at large, therefore I will be the shorter, and with my comendations to your self your wyfe your father in law, your unckle Michell,[11] Robt Seddon[12] and all our good neighbours, will cōmitt you to god and rest

Yours ever Assured

Bay: Castle   NATHAN WALWORTHE.
      Novē 29, 1623.

[5] '*my Lord's consent,*' *i.e.*, William, sixth earl of Derby, as lord of the manor of Pilkington, taken from the Pilkington family, who were Yorkists, by Henry VII., and given to the first earl of Derby, whose descendants still hold it.

[6] '*Mr. Langley.*' John Langley, who succeeded his father, William Langley, as rector of Prestwich in May 1611. He was also rural dean of Manchester. He died in August 1632, and was buried at Prestwich.

[7] '*The other side.*' The chapel stands on the Outwood side of the river Irwell, Kersley being on the opposite bank.

[8] '*James Ouldam.*' He afterwards gave great umbrage to Nathan by his unwillingness to pay his promised contribution to the chapel. See No. 18, &c.

III. — *Addressed To my vary loving frend Peter Seddon
in the Owtwoode.*

Neighbour Peter, I thanke you for your lrē and for your good
newes of my cosins marigge,[13] but especiallye for puttinge me
in hope that some good Northern wynd may blow some of you
to London, whom I shall be glad to see, and in hope thereof will
omitt to wryte any thinge of that cheife business, and onelyc tell
you that the Parliament[14] is put off till the 15 of March and
Count Mansfield[15] is gone wᵗ all his Trayne wᶜʰ is all the newes
we have, when I heare more, you shall heare more, in the meane
tyme wᵗ 1000 comendations to your self and your wyfe, and your
father in law, I comīt you to god and rest

Assuredlye yours

Bay; Castle   NATHAN WALWORTHE.

    feb; 3, 1624.

[9] '*Mr. Murrey.*' Probably George Murray, appointed rector of Bury the year
before. See No. 9.

[10] '*my brother.*' Peter Walworth, Nathan's younger brother, who died in 1626.

[11] '*Michael Seddon,*' younger brother of Raphe Seddon. In his Will, proved at
Chester in 1638, he desires to be buried at Prestwich, "between the great church-
door on the south side, and the little chancel door, being the place of my ancestors'
burial." He devised land in Pilkington to 'neighbour' Peter for life, and then to his
God-son Ralph, Peter's second son, and left legacies to Peter's children, and to the
four children of William Hulton, then minister at Ringley, who had married his niece
Dorothy. See No. 27 and note.

[12] '*Rob't Seddon*' of Kersley, afterwards one of the trustees of Ringley chapel. In
his Will, proved in 1670, he bequeaths "18 of my best silver spoons amongst his three
daughters." He devised his land at Farnworth to his eldest son Robert, who was an
intimate friend of William Hulme, the founder of the Hulmeian exhibitions, and as
such was examined, after Mr. Hulme's death in 1691, as to the real intentions of the
testator.

[13] '*my cosins marigge.*' See No. 8.

[14] '*Parliament is put off.*' Nathan was misinformed; it met 19 February and sat
till 29 May.

[15] '*Count Mansfield.*' He had been allowed to raise 12000 men in England to aid
Frederick the Elector Palatine (king James's son-in-law) against Spain. The troops
were hastily embarked in crowded ships, and lost nearly half their number through
sickness. Ernest de Mansfeld, one of the greatest generals of the seventeenth century,
was the natural son of Count Pierre-Ernest. He learned the art of war under his

IV. — *Addressed To my honest frend and Neighbour
Peter Seddon, in the Owtwood.*

Neighbour Peter, I marvayle how you may yeeme,[16] after so
longe and hard a winter, to be so long from the plough, as to
wryte so longe a lre̅, not that I thinke it so longe, either for
matter or manner, if it were a quyre of paper more, but I must
needs Confess myself, so much the more beholdinge unto you,
that will spare so much tyme, frō better Imployment, but to
leave Complementinge, and goe to a more Serious busines, I
hope there needs no more to be said, but to goe forward, I have
sent some money to begin with, and more you shall have before
you need it, but I must be A Sutor to you, that seeinge my
brother[17] cañot be about it, by reason of other busines for his
Daughter, but hath comitted it to his Se̅ñe, whose experience in
those things is yet but greene, that you would Ioyne wᵗ him, and
ayde him, that the worke may goe the better forward for two
eyes see more than one, and two heads are better then one, I
Doubte not, but all good neyghbours, will be willinge and readye

---

brother Charles in Hungary and then served in Flanders, and afterwards with the
Bohemians in their struggle against Austria.   The Bohemians having chosen the
Elector Palatine as their king, Count Mansfeld rendered him good service, both in
the field and by undertaking missions to France and England to solicit aid.   In 1626
Mansfeld was defeated by the famous Wallenstein, and soon after resigned his command to the duke of Saxe.   Falling ill in November of the same year, while on a
journey to Venice, and feeling his end approaching, the count put on his uniform and
expired, leaning on two servants.   Mansfeld was as distinguished in diplomacy as in
war ; patient, indefatigable, and fertile in resource, he compelled even his enemies to
admire him.   The following anecdote is told of his generosity : Being informed that
Cazel, one of his officers, betrayed his plans to the enemy, he gave him 300 rix-dollars
with a letter to the Austrian commander to this effect ; "Cazel being your devoted
servant and not mine, I send him to you, that you may profit by his services."

[16] '*yeeme*,' or yeme, means to *care* ; to give *attention* ; also to take care, as

"His browe stank for defaut of yeme."

Beves of Hamptoun, p. 62.

"Ant to Moyses, the holy whyt
The hevede the laws to yeme rhyt."

Harrowing of Hell, p. 15.

[17] '*my brother*,' *i.e.*, Peter Walworth.

to further it, but I would have you in a more speciall manner to
take some Care about it, both because you are neere, and have
more understandinge then some others and may more convenientlye meet often and Conferr together, I wish no more hurt
to your neighbour Barton,[18] then fowre hares more to breed in
his Orchard thro March, nor worse lucke to befall the two Parsons,[19] then such as the former hunters had that I may laugh at
them a little, I was no such a hunter, when I was amonge you,

for Robert Seddon, I desyre to looke no further, neither doe I
resolve upō any other, if he be not too little, or too high as we
say, All the newes[20] is you must skoure your Armour and whett
your sworde, but for this I referr you to my brothers lrē for I am
starke tyrde, farewell,

Assuredlye yours

Bay: Castle   NATHAN WALWORTHE.
    Mar: 25, 1624.

V.— *Addressed To my lovinge frend Peter Seddon in y^e
Owtwoode.*

Neighbour Peter, I thanke you for your lrē, especiallye for
that part wherein you give me good encouragement, that the
worke shall be accepted, and give good Content, for that is my
Desyre whatsoever it Cost me, I stand now on thornes till I
come and see it, wch will be w^in this month or there abouts, w^ch
will be a good tyme to goe a fishinge,[21] provyde good rods,

[18] '*Bartin.*' Nicholas Bartin, a yarn merchant, carrying on business in Manchester
in 1649, but residing in Pilkington. [R.S.S.]

[19] '*the Parsons,*' *i.e.*, of Prestwich and Bury. (See No. 9, and note.)

[20] '*the newes.*' This refers to the war with Spain, declared 10 March.

[21] '*goe a fishing.*' Mr. Bailey suggests that Nathan probably fished for eels, for
which the Irwell was once famous. Thus James Cheetham of Smedley, writing about
fifty years later, says, "neither are the inhabitants on its banks partial by reason of
their vicinity; but it [*i.e.*, the Irwell eel] is highly applauded for its excellent taste by
persons mere strangers and such as had the estimation of curious palates; and having
often enquired of the neighbouring people to it what might be the reason they have
unanimously ascribed it to the numerousness of fulling mills that stand on that river,
and say that the fat, oil and grease scoured out of the cloth make the eels palatable
and far above other river eels." (Anglers' *Vade Mecum*, 1681, p. 179.)

hooks, and lynes, and then lett me alone, let there not be
wantinge 2 or 3 hares nether, that Idlenes may be Avoyded,
and so I leave the rest till I come my self, the kinge[22] was
crowned yesterday, and many Knights of the Bathe[23] were
made, to name them would be too longe, the Parliament begins
on Monday next, this is all the newes I have, So desyringe to be
remembred to your fatherinlaw, to Robt̄ Seddō, to Ellis Smith
to your self and your wyfe, and your Unckle Michill, I comĩtt
you to god and rest

                                     Assuredlye yours
Bay: Castle   NATHAN WALWORTHE.
febr ; 3 ; 1625.

———

VI. — *Addressed To my very loving frend Peter Seddon
in the Owtwoodes in Pilkingtō.*

Neighbour Peter, my pillow and I had longe before resolved
of the certayntye of my Iorney that morninge, although I speake
somewhat doubtfullye unto you to prevent such solemne leaue-
takings, as usuallye doth more afflicte then in any way ease the

---

[22] '*The kinge was crowned.*'   Charles succeeded to the throne 27 March 1625, and
was crowned the following February.

[23] '*Knights of the Bath.*'   So called, of course, because originally they were washed
on the eve of the ceremony.   I have not met with any detailed account of this curious
custom, but we read of "Sir Walter Dennys of Gloucestershire, who was made a
knight *by bathing* at the creation of Arthur Prince of Wales in November 1489."
Cervantes, writing in 1605, makes Don Quixote, on the eve of being dubbed knight
by the Innkeeper, watch his armour, which he had placed on a cistern close to a well ;
but it does not appear that the Don actually took a bath.   Henry IV. made forty-six
esquires, "who had watched all night and bathed themselves," knights of the bath,
on the day he was crowned, and the precedent was followed at succeeding coronations
up to that of Charles II. in 1661. (See Evelyn's *Diary*, 19 April 1661.)   The order
then fell into abeyance till revived by George I. in 1725.   On the occasion to which
Nathan refers, sixty-eight knights were created.   The full list may be found in Guillim's
Display of Heraldry, ed. 1724, p. 223.   The steward took a special interest in the
ceremony, because William earl of Pembroke was joint commissioner with Thomas
earl of Arundel to make knights of those persons as the king should call to that dig-
nity (Collins's *Peerage*, edit. Brydges, vol. iii, pp. 123, 124), and Philip Herbert
was the third knight on the list, which also includes Sir Charles Stanley.

harts of partinge frends; I am sory it was your luck to come into Ringley in such a disastrous tyme; but I could not help it, when I come agayne I will make you all wearye of me;

heere is no newes nor no talke, but of the Duke,[24] many fowle matters are alleadged agaynst him, by both the houses, but the ki: sticks to him still; and two have beene comitted to the Tower for speakinge agaynst him Sᵣ Dudley Diggs,[25] and Sᵣ Jo: Eliott, but Sᵣ Dud: Diggs is out agayne, but the other is not, much Adoe there is, and what will be the end, we know not yet, I have written to my brother about the disposinge of some things in the Chappell, I referr you to his lr̄e; and thus wᵗ comēndations to your self, and to your second self, to your father in law, Wᵐᵉ Seddon[26] Robte Seddō and all their wyves, to the Scoolemayster and all the Scollers, and let him ever remember the saying of plut: vt Ager si non colatur, non solum Infrugiferus manet, verū etiam multa Silvestria producit.   Ita Adoloscens Rationis capax nisi preceptis honestis exerceatur, nō solū nō evadat bonus sed ad multa vitia, deflectetur, and that of Plin: vrsus Informes gignit catulos, eos tamen lambendo format, ita rudē Ingenij foetū diutina cura expoliri convenit pli: li: 8 c: 26 and let the Scollers remember the Answere that Diogenes made to one that asked quod onus terra gravissimū Sustineret? Indoctum Hominem, I will trouble you with no more, but leave you to gods protection and rest

Assuredlye yours

Bay: Castle   NATHAN WALWORTHE

May 18, 1626

forget me not to Mᵣ fox,[27] and tell him his soñe is well, I was with him yesterday.

---

[24] '*the Duke.*' If Nathan had written thirty years ago, this phrase would have meant the great duke of Wellington; one hundred and thirty years ago, it would probably have meant William, duke of Cumberland, the victor at Culloden; but in 1626, Nathan could only refer to George, duke of Buckingham, at that time the only duke in the three kingdoms: a fact which may partly explain Buckingham's inordinate pride.

VII.— *Addressed To my very lovinge frend Peter Seddon in the Owtwoods*

Neighbour Peter, I thanke you for taking such paynes in so fully relatinge the manner of my Brother's Departure,[28] it is a [Consolation] to ye livinge, to have a good testimonye [of] their frends behaviour, In their sicknes, and [death] and it will make them Crye with Baalam ; O let me dye the Death of the righteous &c: Num: [23. 10] I little thought, but that he should have hard this newes of me, and not I of him, but god hath not yet sufficientlye humbled me, but will let me see more Care and Sorrow, but I will not harpe upō this stringe, nor greeve that he is happy but expect w^t longinge the tyme of myne owne dissolution,

---

[25] '*Diggs and Elliott.*' Sir Dudley made some submission and was released immediately. Sir John was confined in the tower for eight days.

[26] '*Wm Seddon.*' Perhaps neighbour Peter's brother, or William Seddon of Farnworth, who, in July 1631, signed a "quaint peticon of the inhabitants of the Chappelrie of ffarnworth" to the mayor of Chester, complaining of the misgovernment of Farnworth Grammar School (see *Harl. MSS.* 2103, f. 174). Nathan's letter concludes with an amusing display of learning, perhaps intended more for 'neighbour' Peter than for the 'scoolemayster.'

[27] '*Mr. fox.*' Probably Thomas Foxe of Whitfield in Pilkington, Peter's uncle. He was the third son of William Foxe of the Rhodes (who bequeathed him, in his Will, "my little bay nagg"), and grandson of John Foxe of Toxteth Park, who married Jane, daughter and coheiress of —— Parr of Rhodes. Thomas Foxe was present at the consecration of the chapel as Lord Derby's agent ; and in December 1636 he was employed by Lord Strange to transfer the Stanley Chapel, in the Collegiate Church in Manchester, to the warden and fellows, to be used as a library (see *Tanner MSS.* in the Bodleian Library quoted in "Local Gleanings" for March 1876). In 1641-2 Thomas Foxe, "gentleman," was one of those who took the Protestation. He married first, Alice Nuttall of Bury ; and secondly, Grace Northern, who survived him. For a full account of the Foxe family see *Stanley Papers* (pt. ii, p. 109), edited by Canon Raines. In Donald Lupton's *History of the Moderne Protestant Divines*, 8vo, 1637, p. 277, it is said of John Foxe, the martyrologist, that "hee was born in the county of *Lancaster.* His young yeeres shewed that hee was layd out for a Scholler, and so he had education accordingly in a famous Schoole."

[28] '*my brother*,' *i.e.*, Peter Walworth of Ringley Fold, who left two sons, Ellis and Nathan, and three daughters, Sarah, Hester, wife of William Wilson of Poppithorne, and Mary, wife of Hugh Parr of Kersley.

The parliament[29] is ended, the ki: will not have the Duke to fall, the kingdome shall perish rather, the earle of Bristow is sent to the Tower, all the Scaffolds, and pageants are puld downe that were erected, for the ki: goinge through Londō, there will be no show, this is all the newes, whereof let your father[30] and Robīc Seddon be partakers because I cannot wryte to them now, and thus wᵗ commendations to your self and your wyfe, and to them, and to Michill, &c, I comͥitt you to god and rest

Assuredlye yours

Bay: Castle   NATHAN WALWORTHE.
June, 16, 1626.

VIII.

Neighbour Peter, blame not me that you have hard frō me no sooner, your lrē Dated July 4, came to my hands but now this 3 of Aug: as soone as I recᵈ it I begin to Answere it, which although I can not doe in that largnes that yours requyrs yet I will say somethinge as breiflye as I can,

1, what I said to my Cosin in such a place was upon some reasons wᶜʰ I gave him then, but now I utterlye disclayme from them,

2, you say I restrayne frō one but provyde not an other; if I had lived in the Cuntry; and had beene Accquaynted, it may be I would,

3, I dislyke not the 3 properties wᶜʰ you say fittlye doe Agree in [these two]

4, I commende not my Cosin for bearinge hir in hand a prentishipp at least, and not resolving in all that tyme, wᶜʰ (as you say) hath hindred hir frō better preferment, but how is that proved?

---

[29] '*The Parliament.*' Lord Bristol had accused Buckingham of being the cause of the war with Spain, and the commons petitioned Charles to remove the duke from his council, but the king dissolved Parliament (June 15) and so prevented the presentation of a remonstrance reiterating the charge.

[30] '*your father.*' Nathan must mean Peter's father-in-law, William Seddon, as Raphe Seddon died in 1612.

5 To Satisfye the godlye is well, to stopp the mouths of ye wicked is good, but what care I what the wicked say, if my Conscience speake not against me, or Checke me,

6, farr be it from me that I should Advyse my Cosin, to refuse this, in hope of greater portion,

7. and lastly Be it knowne unto all men by these presents that I Nathan Walworth of Londō gent: Doe heereby declare and publish to ye world that I give my free and full Consent, that my Cosin Ellis shall marry Alice Parr[31] (for so I thinke her name is) if they two be so Agreed, and this I thinke is sufficient and they may beleeve me, for I thinke I was the first man that named the matter to the old woman, by the same token that I called hir into the Barne to bye A fatt Calfe,

if it be obiected that since I have seemed to be Contrary, it is true, but I have Disclaymed frō those reasons in my first Article.

I am sory I cannot so fullye Answere every particular as I would, but verbū sapient: sat est, my La:[32] is now removinge into ye Cuntry and I am full of busines, and more sory that ye Caryer hath played the knave, in keepinge your lrē till now, and made you to expect an answere so longe, for I doe Assure you, I received it but now,

for Mr Fox his busines, let him send his Daughter upp, I will Doe what I can, and also for his soñe, I neither have roome nor leasure to wryte comendations to my frends, you must Supply that, and I wil be yours

NATHAN WALWORTHE.

Bay: Castle
    Aug: 3, 1626.

---

[31] 'Alice Parr,' a relative of Hugh Parr of Kersley.

[32] 'my La:,' i.e., Mary, wife of William, third earl of Pembroke, and eldest daughter and coheiress of Gilbert, seventh earl of Shrewsbury. Lord Clarendon says that this earl of Pembroke had but an ill bargain of her fortune when he took with it her crooked person and disposition.

IX. — *Addressed To my lovinge frend and neighbour*
Peter Seddon in the Owtwood.

Honest Neighbour, your last l^r̄e was so welcome to me, that I
am trobled that I had not then, nether have now tyme to Answere it so fully as I would for by it I know that to be brought
to passe which I have so long Desyred and now I am at peace
with my self and with all the world and care for no more, onelye
whyle I live I desyre to heare that as there hath beene so good
a begininge so I may heare no other but that you all agree, and
Draw one way, least by faction and Scisme all be mard[33] agayne,

Your day of meetinge was fittlye Chosen, and so great a number putts me in mynde of what the poet said Spectatum veniunt,
venuint spectentur vt ipsi,[34] for I make no question but some
came to see, and to be seene and to leayrne newes rather then
to heare and to be edifyed   .   .   .   .   bids me hope the best,
therefore I say no more,

All the recompence I can make those maydes that brought
rushes,[35] is, to wish them good husbands, and if I knew when, I

---

[33] '*mard.*'   " Ire, envy and despair
          Marred all his borrowed visage." — *Milton.*

[34] '*Spectatum,*' &c.   Ovid *Ars. Amat.,* vol. i, p. 99.

[35] ' *Those mayds that brought rushes.*'   This alludes to the well-known Lancashire
custom of " rush-bearing," which has been traced back to the time of Pope Gregory
the Great, who is said to have directed the Saxon converts to Christianity to comme-
morate the dedication of their churches by building huts of boughs and celebrating the
day with a feast.   The pope probably wished to supersede a heathen custom, already
prevailing, by a Christian festival, based on the Jewish feast of tabernacles, just as
Easter takes its name from Eostre, the Saxon Venus, whose festival was celebrated in
April.   Possibly the sort of cone or obelisk into which the rushes are plaited may be
the last vestige of the booths which our ancestors used to construct on these occasions.
The Puritans discouraged the rush-bearing, as savouring still of Paganism, but king
James, in his proclamation against Puritans and Precisians, issued at Hoghton Tower
in August 1618, decreed that women should have leave to carry rushes to decorate the
churches according to their old custom.   As time went on the religious character of
the rush-bearing disappeared, and the main object of the festival, as on this occasion,
was to provide the earthen floor of the churches with a fresh carpet of rushes for the
winter, and this was the custom at Newton Heath as late as 1815.   Now that rushes
are no longer used as carpets, the connection of rush-bearing with the church is alto-

would Dance at their weddings, and the lesse doe I pittie those
that stayd at home, and could not keepe their meate from burn-
inge, by the longe stay of their wished for guestes. in the number of your ministers, I nether fynd Mr. Murrey,[36] Mr. Horrax,[37]
nor Mr. Rawbone [38] whereof I writt in my Cosins lrē the last
weeke, therefore I shall not neede to troble you, to give a reason
of their Absence for he will Doe it, but one thinge I shall for my
Satisfaction, desyre to know of you, and that is why Robt Seddon
is placed above your father in law, and not onelye so, but also
above Jo: Horrax and Wiłłme Hulme,[39] for so I fynd him by
this note, I envye no man for their place, but onelye Desyre to
know a reason now for Mr. Richard Crompton,[40] I . . . a
lrē to him with myne owne hands, wᶜʰ was sent from his sister

gether lost, and the rush-cart goes round the parish and collects the coin of the sym-
pathising by-standers, with the public-house as the ultimate goal of the procession.
The festival Nathan here mentions seems to have taken place on St. Martin's day
(11 November), but in most parishes it was held in the third week of August. Booker
(writing in 1852), says that rush-bearing was discontinued at Prestwich within the last
twelve years, but at Newton Heath it retains its popularity, and at Bowness and Am-
bleside young girls still hang up wreaths in the church to remain till the next year.
(See *Notes and Queries* for 1876, and *Local Gleanings* for August 1875.)

[36] '*Mr. Murray.*' George Murray, B.D., of King's College, Cambridge, who had
been tutor to Lord Strange. In August 1622, Lord Derby presented him to the
rectory of Bury, where he died in March 1633.

[37] '*Mr. Horrox.*' Alexander Horrocks, vicar of Deane, who fell under the censure
of Laud about this time. He was afterwards in great danger during the "Bolton
massacre," when Prince Rupert's soldiers cried, "O that we had that old rogue Horrocks that preaches in his grey cloake." Dr. Ormerod (*Civil War Tracts*) mentions
two other ministers of the name ; John Horrocks of Colne, and Thomas Horrocks of
Malden, in Essex, who was also from Bolton. Nathan Walworth was connected with
this family, as a John Horrocks of Pilkington married Sara Wallworthe at Prestwich
in June 1627, and Nathan bequeathed 10/. to "John Horrox the younger."

[38] '*Mr. Rawbone.*' Probably William Rathbande, "clerk" of Blackley in 1631.
(See note by Canon Raines to *Notitia Cest.*, vol. ii, p. 80.)

[39] '*William Hulme*' of Hulme, in Reddish, father of William Hulme the founder.
He had a house in Outwood, and in his will, proved at Chester December 1637, he
bequeathed 20s. to "Maister Hulton now minister at Ringley," and 5/. towards the
endowment of the chapel.

[40] '*Mr. Richd. Crompton.*' Evidently in London at this time. Probably one of
the Cromptons of Breightmet.

in law, it was a good lr̄e, and well written, she read it in my
hearinge, wherin she moved him for some Contribution, and he
promissed to give x^l, but it is out of a Debt wch he hath in that
Cuntry, I told him if the debt were it was well, but if it be
Desperate, then no thankes to him to give that which he cannot
gett himself, but I thinke he will be as good as his worde, as for
Raph Robinson [41] I have not seene him yett but I am sure you
are not so good as your word for you promissed I should have
the notes of ye Sermons [42] this weeke, and you have fayled, and
I am lyke a great bellyed woman y^t long and am lyke to mis-
carye for want of my longinge, and thus with my com̄endations
to your father in law and mother, to Ro: Seddon and his wyfe,
and all in Ringley and the Owtwood, I com̄itt you all to god's
protectiō and rest,

Your lovinge frend

Bay: Castle   NATHAN WALWORTHE.
   No: 23, 1626.

----

*X.— Addressed To my very loving frend Peter Seddon in y^e
Owtwoode of Pilkington.*

Neighbour Peter, you think longe ere you have an Answere of
your business, blame not me, for I have had many a fowle
Jorney about it, and yet cannot effect it, but am still put off
my Lo:[43] is full of busines, but I will speake w^t him tomorrow,
and, I will tell him you have beene heere   I came frō thence
but now, and am afrayde y^e   will be gone therefore I must be
short, I have had some speech w^t ye officers, about ye trees in
and they have promissed I shall have them, my request to
you is that you will goe up to John Horrax and you two take
Mr Tho. fox[44] with you, and view them, and give an estimate of

----

[41] '*Raph Robinson*' of Kearsley, whose daughter Elizabeth married William Hulme
the fonnder. (Dugdale's *Visit. in* 1664.)

[42] '*ye Sermons,*' *i.e.*, the sermons preached at the opening of the chapel.

[43] '*my Lo:.*' Philip, earl of Pembroke (see Introduction).

[44] '*Mr. Tho. fox.*' See No. 6 and note.

them under your hands what they are worth, and send it me, and by it I shall agree with the officers for so they are content, I make no doubt but you will Deale for me as if it were your owne case, and so I am content, and upon your relatiō (for I named you three) I shall make an end wᵗ them onelye this Itē[45] be to you in particular, Deale not wᵗ me as one in the world hath done, And for your busines, I will give them little rest, till it be done, farewell,

Yours, NATHAN WALWORTH.

febr: 27, 1628.

XI.

Neighbour Peter, after you were gone, when I had considered the lrē that came frō Ro: Seddō I was sory that your stay was so short that I could not give an Answere by word of mouth, for there be many things that a man may deliver by word, which a man cannot so well deliver in wrytinge and besyds I am loth, and it is not fitt that she seene in it, or meddle with it, I have written an Answere a weeke Agoe, but I fayled of caryage, and therefore I send it now by Tomy Parr,[46] you need not feare the law, if you be put to it, I say no more referr you to my lrē,

I sent all things the last weeke except raysins[47] currens and prunes, wᶜʰ I would not send because they were not new, for we shall have new before you will have occasion to use them, and the old I did not lyke, and thus wᵗ commendations to your wyfe and thanks for my cheese I comīt you to god and rest

Your lovinge frend

Bay: Castle   NATHAN WALWORTHE
No: 29, 1630

---

⁴⁵ '*this Itē*,' *i.e.*, this hint.

⁴⁶ '*Tomy Parr*,' a trustee of the chapel fund, and one of four who rode over to Lever to escort Bishop Bridgeman to the consecration (See Nos. 24 and 59).

⁴⁷ '*raysins*,' &c., *i.e.*, for Christmas pudding and cakes and mincemeat. About seven years after the date of this letter the Lancashire carriers put up at the Bear Inn in Bassinshaw, London. There the Bolton and Manchester carriers lodged on Thursdays and Fridays. See Sir John Taylor's *Carrier's Cosmography*, 1637. [J.E.B.]

XII.—*Addressed To my lovinge frend Peter Seddon in the Owtwoode.*

Neighbour Peter, why, what's the matter? hath the palsye taken your hand? or is it for want of paper? if I thought so, I would send you some, or is it the Goute? or what els? O, no, now I know what it is, you never received my letter, if you had, you would either have acknowledged the receipt, or have reproved what had beene Amisse in it, all the remedye, and Amends y^t I now can have is to send no more lr̃es by y^t caryer, and so an end of that Songe,

I received a lr̃e, fr̃o my Cosin Ric: Hardman,[48] and he Assures me that the Tythe was better then 20*l.* this last yeare, I have written unto him agayne that if either he or any one or two Joyned with him, will enter into band to pay 20*l.* per añ̃ the B. B.[49] shall have his demand, and he, or they shall have a lease for 21 yeares, I have writt that corne beinge deare this last yeare it may be there might be made 20*l.* and yet an other yeare, it may not be worth 16*l.* howsoever I would have you not to omitt so good oportunitie, for a fitter thinge then this cannot bee but talk with your father,[50] and Robte and others, and learne ye Just valew, and if you can fynd it, (Com̃unibus annis)[51] worth 19 or 20*l.* a yeare, he shall have 200*l.* for it, for I have done what I can, and I perceive he will not be drawne to abate any thinge of 200*l.* the sooner you dispatch it ye better it will be, if you goe 3 or 4 of you to Bolton, and talke w^t Rich: Hardm̃a he will help you what he can, so I rest, yours,

NATH: WALWORTHE.

Bay: Castle
May, 2, 1631.

---

[48] '*Ric: Hardman*' of Radcliffe Bridge, said to have been converted by John Angier, at this time minister of Ringley (see Heywood's *Life of Angier*).

[49] '*the B. B.,*' *i.e.,* Bishop Bridgeman.

[50] '*your father,*' *i.e.,* Peter's father-in-law. See No. 7 and note.

[51] '*Com'unibus annis.*' Taking one year with another.

XIII.—*Addressed To my very lovinge freud Peter Seddon in the Owtwood of Pilkington.*

Neighbour Peter,

you need not feare the largnes of your lrēs will trouble me, for I am sorye they are no longer, they come not now, as they were wont to doe, lyke Eliah to Ahab 1 Ki: 21, 20, but lyke yᵉ Prodigall sone to his father, Luc: 15, 20 welcome els I could hardlye have spared so much tyme as to have Answered this, hold together as you doe, and I would you had drunke one shillinge more at John Glovers[52] upō my skore, onelye, as I have often sayd stand upō your owne bottome, you are wyser then I and need not my Advyse nor councell, nor protectiō, for if your Case be good, it will bear out it self, if bad I neither can nor will defend it, I thanke you for your lrē and am desyreous to heare of your proceedings, but yet I would not have you to let others know, that you have made me Accquaynted with it, I shall not come as I thought about Bartlemewtyde,[53] it will be Mich: first for ought I know yet, my Cosin Nathan[54] is a busye man I warrant you, but he wants money, if he doe, he must (as I told him) try his Creditt, or myne, or both, for I cannot help him before Allhallentyde[55] or if the worst come to the worst let him goe to the hedge for a stake, but I had not need to stand foolinge heere, that came but home yesternyght late, and have all my busines to doe, and muste goe towards Wilton[56] to morrow ; farewell,

Your lovinge frend

Bay: Castle   NATHAN WALWORTHE.

Aug: 5, 1631.

---

[52] '*John Glovers.*' John Glover of Outwood took the protestation in that township in 1641-2.

[53] '*Bartlemewtyde,*' i.e., August 24th.

[54] '*Cosin Nathan,*' son of Peter Walworth of Ringley, and nephew of Nathan Walworth, who always writes of him as *cousin.* So the king, in *Hamlet,* says to his nephew, "Cousin Hamlet, you know the wager" (*Hamlet,* act v). The word cousin is from the Latin *consobrinus,* corrupted in late Latin into *cosinus,* literally the child of a mother's sister, but in a general sense one collaterally related more remotely than a brother or sister (see *Notes and Queries,* 5 S. vi, p. 75).

XIV.—*Addressed To my very loving frend Peter Seddon in*
ye Owtwood in Pilkington.

Neighbour Peter, Baynards Castle stands where it did and so strong, that it neither feares wynd nor weather, nor Stormes, nor undermyninge, and both owner and Inhabitants as unmoveable as it, unless Atropos, cut the thread of lyfe, Against which there is no resistance, but it would be worth your labour to cast away a little money of that wch you have hoarded up, by being so longe at rest frō Suites[57] and law businesses, and come and see how naked Paules stands,[58] all the houses in Paules church yard pulde downe, and layd levell with the ground, and yet to see hir all glorious within, well repayred and ritchly guilt and adornde, and you may walke about hir (as David sayth) psa: 48 12, marke hir bulwarkes, and tell hir Towers, and this makes me not a little to wonder, and to condemne your backwardnes, (I speake in

[55] '*Allhallontyde.*' All Saints' Day, November 1st.

[56] '*Wilton.*' Lord Pembroke's seat near Salisbury. The steward's former master, Earl William, died on the 10th April 1630.

[57] '*at rest frō Suites.*' The *Calendar to Pleadings* shows that the Seddon family were frequently at law about lands at Kersley and Pilkington, and the right of "digging coal." (Cf. vol. iii, pp. 376, 400, 457, &c.)

[58] '*how naked Paules stands.*' Probably while Nathan Walworth was writing this letter he could see St. Paul's from his 'closet' at Baynard's Castle. The year before (26 March 1631) a Committee was appointed by an Order of the Lords of the Council, with power to compound with the tenants of the houses built about St. Paul's; and another order (2 March 1631-2) gave power to the sheriffs to pull down, if obedience was not yielded. "It cost," says Archbishop Laud, "eight or nine thousand pounds (as appears upon the accounts) merely to take down the houses, (which had no right to stand there), before we could come at the church to repair it" (see Wharton's *Hist. of the Troubles of Archbishop Laud*, pp. 224-45). Laud was active in procuring funds for this restoration. He contributed largely himself, gained help from the universities, and from Sir Paul Pindar and other wealthy laymen, and by the king's permission appropriated to this purpose the fines imposed in the High Commission Court.

Denham (writing in 1643) says of this restoration of St. Paul's,

> " Now shalt thou stand, tho' sword, or time, or fire,
> Or zeal, more fierce than they, thy fall conspire
> Secure, while thee the best of poets sings
> Preserved from ruin by the best of kings."
>   (Cooper's *Hill*, l. 21).

generall) when all ye world sett to their hands to repayre and builde, you will nether build, nor maintayne what is built, your excuse to say nothinge can be found out, is frivolous and vayne, and worse than all ye rest, for I persuade my self, if men were willinge it were Impossible but some thinge might have beene found out ere this, but I say nothinge, Charitie thinketh not evill 1 Cor: 13, 5, and if you have gotten one to your mynd I am glad, the Creditt and the benefyte too, will be your owne, and you can never have a fitter tyme to establish your selves, in as much free-dome and libertie, as now whyle Mr Allen[59] is there, take tyme therefore, and looke about you, *least* "had I wist" come too late, I will ever pray for you, and I can not end better, I am

Your everlastinge frend

Bay: Castle   NATHAN WALWORTHE.
Nov̄ē: 12, 1632.

XV.—*Addressed To my very lovinge frend Peter Seddon in the Owtwoode of Pilkington.*

Neighbour Peter, I must recant my letter wch I sent by Geo: Brooke,[60] for now I see you Indevour to doe somethinge, and although it be but a small thinge, yet it is somethinge, and a small beginninge may bringe on greater matters, I have beene w^t Mr Downes,[61] and showed him your lr̄e, and he wills you to

---

[59] '*Mr. Allen.*' Isaac Allen, M.A., instituted rector of Prestwich, three months before, on the death of John Langley. He married (June 1622) Anne, sister of Edmund Assheton of Chadderton, who gave him the living. Neighbour Peter was his churchwarden in 1643, and two years later was summoned before a commission, with Richard Lomax, Richard Barlow, Hester Wilson, and others, to give evidence against Mr. Allen for his Royalist opinions. Oliver Heywood mentions him as "old Mr. Allen, a solid substantial preacher turned out in the war time for not taking the covenant." He died February 1660, and was buried at Prestwich (Booker's *Prestwich*).

[60] '*Geo. Brooke*' "cozen" to Nathan Walworth, who left him in his Will "fortie shillings."

[61] '*Mr. Downes.*' Probably John Downes of Wardley Hall, who married Penelope, daughter of Sir Cecil Trafford, and died May 1648.

NATHAN WALWORTH AND PETER SEDDON.

come to him at his retorne, and he will send for that Booth,[62]
and give you the best advyce he can, I wish you to follow it,
and not let it slip as you doe alwayes, and then say it was gone
before you came, it is lykely you may have it well worth your
money

you say you have a minister, I am glad of it, god grant he be
no worse than the last,[63] I am so coled, that I cannot wryte any
longer, my fingers are clumst[64] farewell

Yours

Bay: Castle   NATHAN WALWORTHE.
Nove̅: 16, 1632

XVI.—*Addressed To my lovinge frend Peter Seddon in
the Owtwood*

[November xxv[th] 1633]

Neighbour Peter, I have nothinge to wryte [since] I writt by
Robert Lever[65] but onelye [that] I received a lre by this bearer
I [have] let him goe without an other, partlye [to] put you in
mynd to see those breaches [in the] Chappell hedge mended,
and one thinge more [has come] into my head wch I would have
[done] and that is I would have trees sett with[in the] hedge
round about ye Chappell [a reasonable] Distance one from an
other I thinke . . . . will be best, fyne strayght trees cho[sen]
will in tyme make a fyne show, if everye [one] will sett their
helping hand it will soone be [done] and I am sure you have

---

[62] '*Booth.*' John Booth of Farnworth signed the petition to the mayor of Chester
in 1631 with reference to the state of Farnworth school.

[63] '*the last,*' *i.e.*, John Angier, who came to Ringley in 1629, and preached there
for nearly a year. He was then suspended by Bishop Bridgeman and removed to
Denton. (See *An helpe to better Hearts for better times*, by John Angier, Pastor at
Denton, Lond. 1647.)

[64] '*clumst,*' *i.e.*, benumbed ; clumsy.

[65] '*Robert Lever,*' gent., the younger brother of James Lever of Darcy Lever, and a
citizen and clothier of London. He died unmarried, and by Will, dated March 1641,
devised lands in Harwood for erecting and maintaining a free grammar school at
Bolton.

woods[66] round a[bout] you that will yeeld such trees, I leave it
[to] your consideration, if any charges be, I will pay it [I] hope
to have a longe lrē from you and that you haue done that busines with my Lo: Strange,[67] I have done, my fingers ends are so
cold, I can wryte no more, I am,

Your well wishinge frend

[Bay]: Castle   NATHAN WALWORTHE.

[Nov.] 25, 1633.

---

[66] '*woods.*' Hence the name of the district, the "Outwood of Pilkington." Prestolee must have been very prettily situated before coal mines and chemical works
altered the neighbourhood. Whittle calls it "a most romantic spot, forming rich en-
closed land, possessing nemoral scenery and rivulets in abundance; hill and valley
mingle here." He adds, "the name means Priest's lea, being land which belonged to
the oratory at Farnworth"; and he elsewhere tells us, but gives no authority, that the
hermit of Farnworth lived in a wooden hut, and had a croft of land assigned to him by
Arnold de Halsall, for the cultivation of medicinal herbs to distribute as syrups and
ointments. " Presto Wode " is mentioned in a deed, dated 12 Hen. VI., relating to
Prestwich church; and we find " Prestawe als Prestall " in the *Cal. Inq. post Mort.*,
vol. i, p. 78, of the date of 12 Jac. I. As early as 1483, Adam Prestall held land in
Farnworth, adjoining that of John Hulton and Richard Seddon (cf. *Harl. MSS.*,
2112, fol. 166 b), but whether his family gave their name to Prestolee, or *vice versá*, I
will leave the reader to determine.

[67] '*Lo: Strange.*' James Stanley, son and heir of William, sixth earl of Derby;
summoned to Parliament as "Jacobus Stanley de Strange Chevalier" in March 1628;
succeeded as seventh earl in 1642; beheaded at Bolton in 1651. Brown and Whittle,
in their *Histories of Bolton*, mention some local traditions about the "martyr" earl,
which, as their works are very scarce, I may quote here for what they are worth.
Brown says, "from an authority on which we consider reliance may be placed, we have
learned that James, earl of Derby, in his boyhood, was sent to a respectable day
school near the old hall at Rhodes. There lived at that time, at Prestolee, on a large
farm, held of the Derby family on perpetual lease renewable on a small fine, Ralph
Seddon, gentleman. He is represented as being descended from one of the followers
of the Conqueror, serving him as a bowman, and to have lived in a style of rustic
opulence and plenty. Ralph Seddon had twin sons born in 1604." Lord Strange,
then aged about 16, boarded at the house of Ralph Seddon, and became intimate with
his twin sons, who were nearly of the same age, and William, one of the twins,
accompanied the young lord to college. William took orders, and was the first clergy-
man who preached in Ringley chapel. His brother John was reared as a soldier, and
"both took part in the civil wars, and after sharing many perils accompanied their
patron to the scaffold at Bolton." I may remark upon this, that if Lord Strange
lodged at Prestolee, it must have been after the death of Ralph Seddon in 1612. His

XVII.—*Addressed To my very lovinge frend Peter Seddon in the Owtwood of Pilkington.*

Neighbour Peter, now at last, (though [both of] you have played the men, and ended with . . . . . overthwart B. B.[68] who hath put you to a great [deale of] troble, but it is no matter, now it is done [with] good words, and although he thinke the Contrarye, yet he shall see that I will doe somethinge before I Dye unless god prevent me, I am now fuller of busines then ever I was, I have no great hope of cominge downe but betwene this and easter you shall heare more, for my La:[69] lyes here, and I can scarce goe out to pisse, but I hope before easter she will be gone, and then I shall have more libertie, but you need not stire nor take such a foule Jorney, I will sett your land at libertye ere it be longe, I hope you have your band up out of his hands that you entered into for the 100*l.*, that you may have no more to doe with him, I cannot choose but laugh when [I] thinke what a foole he would have made me lyke . . . . . . to enter into bond to him, and tell him what I [wanted] that it might be cryed at the Crosse, yes, I thinke no more of Greenhall,[70] at the uttermost

widow (whose name both Brown and Whittle give incorrectly), as the daughter of Lord Derby's steward, would be a suitable person with whom to entrust the young lord, that he might, as Brown suggests, "strengthen his frame by field-sports." It is doubtful if Lord Strange ever went to college. William Seddon took his degree at Magdalene College, Cambridge, but I have been unable to obtain any evidence that Lord Strange was educated there, as the college authorities have no record of admissions earlier than 1644. Brown elsewhere speaks of the close connection between Lord Derby and the sons of Ralph Seddon, and mentions a curious delft stone jug, from which the earl is said to have drunk some water shortly before his execution. This jug was, for a long time, kept a relic by the Seddons of Little Bolton, and is now in the possession of Alfred Diggles, Esq., of Bramhall.

[68] '*B.B.*,' *i.e.*, Bishop Bridgeman. See Introduction.

[69] '*my La:*' *i.e.*, Anne, countess of Pembroke, mentioned again in No. 41. See Introduction.

[70] '*Greenhall.*' The purchase of Greenhall had apparently been proposed by 'neighbour' Peter as part of the endowment of Ringley Chapel; it was, at this time, rented by Robert Hey, from Mr. Atherton (See Nos. 20 and 38). Thurstan Tyldesley, in his Will, dated September 1547, mentions "y*e* tithes of Wale Bethum Hall and Grenall."

...... hardlye be worth 19*l.* per ann̄ ; and is not worth ......
it goe, I thanke you for your paynes, in ...... the B:ᵖˢ proceedings in the consecration, [It] is now at an end, for a copye of Mʳ
...... it not, you have now Accquittance whereof ...... keepe
a copye, send that Accquittance everye ...... under the ministers
hand of the receipt of 20*s.*, [Green] Hall, and it will be payd unto
the worlds end ...... Adoe, Roger wood⁷¹ is now come for this
...... me wryte no more Comende me to Rob: and farewell
                                        Yours, NA: WA.

Jan: 5, 1634.

XVIII. — *Addressed To my very lovinge frend Peter Seddon
in the Owtwood of Pilkington.*

Neighbour Peter, you have sent the feoffment, and bond how
neighbours stand bound,⁷² but these are not that wᶜʰ I looke for,
that wᶜʰ I lacke is the coppye of the Bᵖˢ Instrument or Act of
Consecration of yᵉ Chapple, wᶜʰ you call heere in your lr̄e the
deed of conservation, this is it wᶜʰ I must have, you may have it
in yᵉ Bᵖˢ Register, send it me as speedelye as you can, these two
things you name are both good ; but you must learne whether
they be holden in Capite, or in Soccage,⁷³ if they be not holden
in Soccage they will doe us no good, they may be called in question heereafter, and the ki: may dispose otherwyse of them, that
of Mr. Ratcliff⁷⁴ at foxdenton I lyke well, and it is worth the
money, if the tenure be good, learne the truth of that, but goe
no further, till I come or send, hasten the Deed of Conservation
(as you call it) by a trustye messinger, Home, Robinson, and

⁷¹ '*Roger Wood.*' See next letter.
⁷² '*how neighbours stand bound.*' Nathan Walworth probably refers to the list of
contributors. (See No. 59.)
⁷³ '*in capite or in soccage,*' *i.e.*, held directly from the king, where the render was
precarious and uncertain, or from some intermediate lord at a fixed service. The
'socmen' were inferior landowners, who, though their tenures were absolutely copy-
hold, yet had an interest equal to a freehold.
⁷⁴ '*Ratcliff.*' Probably Robert Radclyffe of Foxdenton, living in 1642, who died
unmarried.

Ouldam, that are backward in this, I will pray for them, I sent you a lrē by Roger wood of Boulton a weeke agoe, I hope you have rec[d] it, god send you an honest and a good minister, your meanes is so small, you will hardlye gett a good one, yet for his Incouragement tell him from me whosoever he be, I will make it 20*l.* per aññ,[75] with that wch you give, and perhaps better, I say no more till I see the Deed of conservation, but bid you farewell and rest

Your lovinge frend

Bay: Castle   NATHAN WALWORTHE.
Jan: 8, 1634.

XIX.—*Addressed To my very loving frend Peter Seddon in the Owtwood of Pilkington*

Your liberalitie, is Admyred, and shall be written upō the backe syde of my doore with Chalke or a blacke cole, in perpetuā rei memoriam, for sending a whole shillinge at a tyme, I doubte not but you fasted a weeke for it afterwards, it is no matter, we fasted not, nor bought any lands with it, I could not be so bold now in my L[ds] cellor, as I was in Jo: Harryes tyme,[76] for he is out of his place, and put to his pention of 10*l.* a yeare, because he is growne old, this is the lott and portion of Servingmen, and my turne wil be next, and then I must come and live of the parishe if I did a worke of Superogatiō in sendinge Oxford benefactors, was that any hurt? I know the Difference is not great betweene them, but if there be any you have A brother can satisfye you therein,

I am in a good mood now, and am loth to be put out of it w[ch] I should be, if I should harp upon one stringe, which sometymes

---

[75] '20*l.* per ann.' See No. 26, where Nathan Walworth repeats his offer. This stipend seems a scanty one, but during Angier's ministry at Denton (1631-1677), the value of his chapel was under 20*l.* per annum. (See Heywood's *Life of Angier.*)

[76] '*John Harris.*' He had been, I suppose, butler to Lord Pembroke, and had possibly set up as a wine-merchant, for Nathan Walworth left him in his Will 5*l.* and "all my stone bottles and jugges."

I am angrye at, and sometyme I vex and greive at, and that is,
that you are so slacke, and backeward in setlinge some mayntenance upon ye Chappell, you make show as though you were
willinge, and you have been about this, and about that, and I
know not what, but it will never sinke into my head, but if
you were as willinge as you make show of, you might in
8 yeare have procured somethinge, I say no more, I have said
Inough to this bearer, farewell,

Yours

May 26,   NATH: WALW:
1634

XX.

Neighbour Peter in answer of your letter understand I comend
my Lo: BB: for doing as he hath done for he always tould you
that he would never consecrate it till there were means, and till
it wear Consecrated you should not have the free use of it, only
he gave you lycense for a tyme till you could find out something
and he had stayde not only as it is in the Gospel 3 years waiting
for fruit,[77] but twice 3 year and yet you are as backward as ever.
What would you have him to do, unless you be gorded [78] and
whipt and spurd and you will do nothing. But I dare say nothing more les[t] you will say I do nothing but chyde. I have
talked with Robt. Hey [79] about Green Hall and he is one that
can best inform you of it, for he rents it and he sayth it is worth
20*l.* p. ann. but it is but holden in Fee fearms [80] of Mr. Atherton
and within these five or 6 years their is to be pay'd out of it

---

[77] '*waiting for fruit.*' 'Neighbour' Peter compared to the barren fig tree.

[78] '*gorded,*' to gorde, *i.e.*, to 'strike' or 'spur.' (See Wright's *Provincial Dict.*)

[79] '*Robt. Hey,*' the son of Ellis Hey of Monkshall, near Eccles, and Alice, daughter
of Robert Holden of Holden. He married Penelope, fourth daughter of Adam Byrom
of Salford, who survived him. (Dugdale.)

[80] '*Fee farms,*' *i.e.*, Mr. Atherton reserved a rent of at least one fourth of the annual
value. John Atherton of Atherton, whose eldest daughter Margaret married John
Bradshaw of Bradshaw, mentioned below and again in Nos. 21 and 25.

1*l*. 6*s*. 8*d*. to the Lord so that then it will be worth but 18*l*. 13*s*. 4*d*.
I think 15 years purchas is Enough to be payd for it but he
demands 400*l*. because (saith he) there is a fair House upon it
the Building whereof cost near 300*l*. but what are you the better
for that unless it stood neare the Chappell to be short I like the
thing well and you never find any more convenient, all the matter is to work wisely with Mr. Bradshaw he is an honest man
and a man of sufficient and it were nothing for him to give such
a thing for such a use at least to deal favourably and charitable
in it, which you may easily procure him to do if you set wisely
about it.　I have met with Mr. Aynsworth [81] also and he will do
what he can for you and for the 4 nobles [82] to Mr. Atherton he
may be dealt with so as he may part with it upon faverable
terms and then it will be absolutly worth 20*l*. and perhaps more
for Robt. Hey saith if he may have a Lease for 22 years he will
bestow 30*l*. upon it in marling and other Husbandry whereas
having it but from year to year he will bestow nothing upon it.

　Robt. Seddon tould you my Lo: would grant the Chappel
ground but I see nothing but words and now [you] will say you
must weed corn, lead turf,[83] tent hay—and we may not yeeme [84]
to follow any business and that it shall be posted of from one
time to another and never anything done, weel I say no more
but I know what I think and that I will keep to myself and wish
well to my Cuntry and so I leave to God and rest

your Lov^g Fr^d NATHAN WALWORTHE.

Bay: Castle
June 28. 1634.

---

[81] '*Mr. Aynesworth.*'　A Robert Ainsworth was a contributor to Mr. Holland in
1652.　(See No. 64.)

[82] '*four nobles.*'　The noble was current at 6*s*. 8*d*.　It was first struck in the reign
of Edward III., and then called a 'penny of gold,' and afterwards a 'rose noble,'
because stamped with a rose.

[83] '*lead turf*,' 'lead' (from 'lade,' Saxon for load) means to 'cart.'　In the north
they 'lead' coals and almost everything which elsewhere they carry or cart.　(See
Brockett's *Glossary of North Country Words*.)

[84] '*yeeme.*'　(See No. 4 and note.)

E

XXI.—*Addressed To my lovinge frend Peter Seddon in the Owtwood of Pilkington.*

Neighbour Peter, I have rec^d both your lr̄es and when I consider them well, I fynd, in effect, the whole burden of the busines is layd upon my shoulders, and not upon yours els what meane these passages? "your purchase" &c: "fitt for your purpose" &c: "if we can conceive any hope that you may have a fitter match we shall certifye you" &c: "we refer all to your consideration" "expectinge your Answere" &c: heere all lyes upon me, and you know that after ye buildinge of the Chappell, I had no more to doe, but you were to allow mayntenance amonge you, as you promissed before ye B. B: and also gave your hands to me, wch I have to show, but now it is come to this, somethinge must be purchased, and although you have mayntayned a minister, yet to purchase a thinge to that valew that you allowed him, you are not Able, well then, what is to be done? will you fall upō me? will you Spurr the horse that will draw? you are not able to make above 120 or 110*l.*, why then lett Greenchall alone lett it goe, meddle not with it, would you have me to lay out 280*l.*, to purchase it? why doe not you rather trye the gentmen of the cuntrye round about you to see what they will doe for you, and let me alone, and then when you have done what you are able, leave the rest to me, it may be I will doe somethinge, but it shall come of my self, I doe not love to be whipt and spurd to it, but if I were willinge to Joyne w^t you in the purchase of Greenhall,[85] I would not give above 300*l.* for it, it is worth no more, let Mr Bradshaw take his Chapman,[86] and make what he can of it, meddle not with it unless he will take 300*l.*, and if Mr Banister[87] have nothinge but commons for you, let that alone too, and I

---

[85] '*Greenhall.*' See No. 17 and note.

[86] '*his chapman,*' *i.e.*, his "valuer," literally "cheapener."

  "Fair Diomede, you do as chapmen do
  Dispraise the thing that you intend to buy."
                    (*Troiles,* act iv, sc. 1.)

[87] '*Mr Banister.*' Probably Richard Banaster of Okenbottom, in the county of Lancaster, whose daughter, Christian, married William Hulme. See No. 9 and note.

will trye what I can harken out in this Cuntrye, I doe not thinke but I shall heare of somethinge y^t will be better Cheape,[88] heereabouts, So farewell, Yours

NATHAN WALWORTHE.

Aug: 1,
  1634.

one thinge I must put you in mynd of (and it is a shame you should be put in mynd of it) why doe not you send ye Accquitance for ye 20s. to Mr Dunster.[89]

XXII.—*Addressed To my very loving frend Peter Seddon in the Owtwood of Pilkington*

Neighbour Peter, I sent you the Copye of the B. B^s lre[90] and what effect it works, or how it speeds I know not, but I am with chyld[91] till I heare, I hope I have written nothinge that may offend, if I have, I will recant; but wott you what?[92] my boy[93] is gone away from me, I have made a foole of him, and used him too well, and now he knows not himself, he aleadgeth that he hath a desyre to be of some trade, and he will bynd himself prentise but thats not the matter, he is a little too much given to the Pott, and I doe looke narrowlye to him and restrayne him from it, and thats the thinge that troubles him, and when he is gone from me, he thinkes he shall have more libertye, I am sory

----

[88] '*better Cheape.*' Cf. Hakluyt (1552–1616). "Afterwards, perceiving that they might have [oyle] farre *better cheape*" (Hakluyt's *Voyages*, new edition, vol. ii, p. 307).

[89] '*Mr. Dunster.*' Robert Dunster was minister of Littleborough, near Rochdale, in February 1642.

[90] '*the B. B's letter*,' i.e., Nathan's letter to Bishop Bridgeman which Peter praises as "full of pyete and policie." (See No. 24.)

[91] '*I am with child*,' cf. St. Paul, "my little children of whom I travel in birth" (Gal., iv, 19), and No. 44, where Nathan says "your letter hits upon my mind as if you were in my bellye."

[92] '*wott you what*,' cf. "Wot ye not what the Scripture saith of Elias" (Rom., xi, 2).

[93] '*my boy*,' i.e., servant.

for him, I have taken a great deale of paines to bringe him up,
and make fitt to serve, and now I am well requyted for my
labour ; I feare his mother will be troubled to heare it, I am
called away, I must be gone, farewell,

                              Your poore frend
Bay: Castle   NATHAN WALWORTHE
  Oct: 4. 1634

XXIII.—*Addressed To my very lovinge frend Peter Seddon
          in the Owtwood of Pilkington*

leave this w^t Mr Richard Lomax[94] in Manchester, and Desyre
him to hyre one to cary this, speedelye and the partye shall pay
ye messinger.

Neighbour Peter, yours of the first heereof I rec^d on Saturday
at night and because you thinke you may have an Answere by
Thursday, (wch I feare will hardlye be) I have sett pen to paper
presentlye, Desyring if it be possible to satisfye your expectatiō,
wch is more then you would do for me, for I must gape and stay
and looke for an Answere, and yet have none in six weekes, and
now it is come it is scarce worth the reading for heere is nothinge
but Delayes, I hope his Lo:^pp [95] will remember that upō the
tender of 100*l.*, and your entringe into band he promissed to
consecrate it, but that 100*l.* was too little to rayse 10*l.* per anñ.
well, now you have undertaken by Morgaginge and by bands to
assure 10*l.* per anñ. what hinders now ? is there any more Iniunc-
tions in Que Eliza: tyme to hinder it now ? why was not this
Iniunction spoken of till now ? I am sory you are Driven to

____

[94] '*Mr Richard Lomax*' of Redvales in Bury, married Isabella, second daughter of
James Chetham of Crumpsal, and niece of the founder. In 1645 he was examined
before a commission as to the 'malignant' opinions of Isaac Allen ; and in 1647 he
gave evidence, before the Presbyterian classis, with reference to complaint made
against Toby Furness, the incumbent of Prestwich. He must not be confounded with
Richard Lomax of Bury, who married Helen, daughter of Robert Radclyffe of Radcliffe (Dugdale, and Booker's *Prestwich*).

[95] '*his Lo:pp*,' *i.e.*, Bishop Bridgeman.

Morgage any thinge in this Case, but feare not I will release you, and if I could but heare, that the Chappell were consecrated (I am loth to speake what I will doe) but I will make the meanes better then 10 or 12*l.* either, but till that be done, I Desyre pardon, if I reveale not my Intent, and if this will not Satisffye ; let not my Lo: put it off with, these Delayes, but let him absolutelye say he will not consecrate it, and I, as I have vowed it and dedicated it to god, so I will not alter that, but I will pull it downe, and sell yᵉ timber, and the Stones, and yᵉ money shall be given to yᵉ poore, and so it shall be Gods still, as for the matter of approbation of yᵉ minister by the parson of Prestw: or Bury⁹⁶ &c: it was ever meant that such a one should be chosen, as should be allowed both for Doctryne and Conformitie, by yᵉ B. B. and all the ministers of yᵉ kingdome,

if the B B Dislyke with any thinge in my former lr̄e, I am sory for it, I writt it in hast, and I sent you the Copye, that you may tell me wherein I have erred, thus have I breiflye written my mynde, If I have omitted any thinge, it is my hast yᵗ causeth it I have sent all about for a messinger, and I heare one Francis Medowerft⁹⁷ goes tomorrow ; by him you shall receive this lr̄e, dated this 7th of Dec: 1634 farewell, Yours

NATHAN WALWORTHE.

———

XXIV.

Good Sʳ ⁹⁸

I have received your Lettʳ of the 7 of December this 27 ⁹⁹ of the same   I thank you for it, for now I see you approve

---

⁹⁶ '*parson of Prestw: or Bury.*' See No. 4 and note.

⁹⁷ '*Francis Medowerft,*' the second son of Richard Medowcroft of Smethurst, in the county of Lancaster, and Jane, daughter and coheir of Gyles Aynesworth of Aynesworth (Dugdale).

⁹⁸ This letter from 'neighbour' Peter to Nathan Walworth describes the consecration of Ringley Chapel. It is interesting to compare this consecration with that of St. Catharine Cree in London just four years earlier, when, if we may believe Prynne, Laud, the bishop of London, entered the church, after he had cried aloud, " Open ye everlasting doors that the king of glory may come in," and fell on his knees with eyes

of y^c Course we hould which Course we are Bound to follow for els y^c BB will doe nothing therfore now may it plase you to know that upon thur^dy the 10 of this instant your Chappel was consecrated and because haply you will expect it therefore I will briefly show you the manner of the BB action and performance of it.

Upon Monday the 7th of this Instant Robt Seddon [100] Thos Parr [1] John Walworth [2] and I went to my Lo. to Lever ; [3] as we had done many a day before ; and Desyred that for the encoragement of you and other well Disposed the Nomination of the Minister might be to you and whom you appointed, we used arguments to perswaid him to it till Certifying him that we did not know that you affected it, but tould him that seeing in all ages those that have been Liberall and Bountifull to pious account have been thought worthie to have the honour of them next God so we thought it was his part to grant and ours to ask the Patronage to you in the Consecration ; but no further prevailed we but that you and the Parson of Prestwich should joyn in the ellection during your life, and after the 3 Parsons of Berry Prest-

elevated and arms extended, and said, " This place is holy." He several times took up from the floor some of the dust and threw it into the air. Approaching the commune table he made many lowly obeisances and gently lifted up the corner of the napkin in which the bread was placed ; beholding the bread he suddenly let fall the napkin, drew back a step or two and bowed three several times towards the bread. Peeping into the cup and beho'ding the wine, the bishop started back and bowed as before. (See Hook's *Life of Laud.*)

[99] '*this 27th.*' There is some error here, as Peter dates his letter on the 14th.

[100] '*Robt. Seddon.*' (See No. 2 and note.)

[1] '*Thos. Parr.*' An original trustee of the chapel fund. He was probably one of the Parrs of Kersley, connected both with the Walworths and Seddons.

[2] '*John Walworth*' of Ringley, a relative of Nathan, who mentions him with some contempt in his last letter to 'neighbour' Peter. He contributed to the Chapel fund and to the maintenance of Mr. Holland in 1653. In August 1647 he and Peter Seddon were examined and approved as elders of Ringley at the Manchester 'classis.' Henry Newcome thus writes of him in July 1658, " I was sent for to Ringley to visit one John Walworth that had been a professor, but had sadly disgraced his profession by drinking." (See Newcome's *Autobiography.*)

[3] '*my Lo: at Lever.*' Bishop Bridgeman was then residing on his estate at Great Lever, where he had built a house and chapel.

wich and Middleton, and further he tould us he would goe towards Chester upon friday and therefore must ether come upon
Thursday or not at all untill Lent, well we hoping of your good
acceptance agreed to him for Thursday, made the Indenture of
Bargin and sale readie a Copy where of you shall receive either
now or by the first convenient messenger ; Thursday being come
proved could frost and Snow and the forenamed 4 men went to
Lever and found my Lo. was not well yet ; in the afternoone the
sune shining forth, he got on horse and came with us with his
retinew and no sooner looked up at the Foxriding gate,[4] but
with an asavaration he saide it was a faire and Butifull House,
we brought him to your house [5] and into your Chamber which
Martha had deckt up and their was provided some modium [6] of
wine and Banketing stuff but my Lord having been troubled
with a loosness the Night before would not drink ; only put upp
some sugar Cake or such like but I warrant you nothing was
Left, so then putting on his Surplice hood or banner habit and
all his Robes, he went to the Chappel gate which was sett oppen,
and there my Uncle Fox. in my Lo Darbys name and your Cosin
Nathan in your name, by a writing then read, did surrender up
both Soyle and Building[7] to the BB by him to be dedicated and
Consecrated for the Service of Almighty God, and then they came
forth the B entered taking a kind of psession and sessin [seizin]

---

[4] '*Foxriding gate.*'   Probably near the top of Stoneclough brow, where the bishop,
riding from Lever, would look down over the valley of the Irwell, where Ringley lies.

[5] '*ye house.*'   The house at Ringley fold, where Nathan Walworth was born.
'Martha' was the widow of Ellis Walworth, younger son of Nathan's brother Peter.
In his Will, dated 2 December 1630, Ellis Walworth directed that a lease of the farm
should be taken in Nathan's name as trustee for his infant daughters, and he appointed
Nathan overseer of the will, and his widow and brother Nathan executors.   He also
left Mr. Langley and Mr. Angier 5*s*. each, "entreating one of them to preach at my
funeral."

[6] '*some modium.*'   Peter means, and perhaps wrote, some 'modicum.'   Cf.

"What modicum of wit he utters."

Shakespeare's *Troil. and Cress.*, act ii, sc. 1.

[7] '*soyle and building.*'   Mr. Fox (see No. 6 and note) represented Lord Derby the
owner of the 'soyle,' and Nathan (see No. 13), his uncle Nathan Walworth.

for that use by such like words. I do accept of this Surrender
and have entered. and then the great South Chappel Dooer
being opened my Lo: stood before it with an awdible voyce
prayed in sentences gathered forth of the Psalms and other Scrip-
tures for the Blessing of the Lord upon them that had done that
pyous work and all those who had been helpers and furtherers of
it, and Cursses execcracions upon those that should deface those
Buildings or diminish those giftes given to that pious use ; and
then entering the Chappel he shut the Dooer, and after a while
oppened it and bad come in and then going into the Reading
Desk he read Evening prayers with certen celected psalms and
Chapters as the 84 ye 122 ye 132 psalm, the 2 of Chro: 6 and
Math. 22 and then read the Letanie with divers addisions for the
occation, and then going to the great Chancell window he sat
down and read the deed of Consecration in Latin wherein he
hath named the Chappell De Sanctitate Domine [8] as I understand it so soone as we have it you shall have a Copy of that
too, and when he had read this then saying let us pray and
kneeling downe [9] at the upper end of the table with his face
down the Chappel before all the Congregation he prayed a long
prayer full of pithie saisonable Petitions like that of Solomon at
the dedication of the Temple ending the same with the Blessing
at the departure and so ended all the Ceremonie in all which I
saw nothing but Godly Lawful and Expedient without anie superstition howsoever some Calumniaters have spoken against this
way, but I think it is because they Love not Bishops, so all being
ended we brought my Lo. to Parr fowld [10] for thither he walked
on foot, and then 2 of us tooke horses and brought him almost

[8] '*de sanctitate domine*' (*sic*). Peter had probably heard the phrase 'de sancto
Salvatore,' as the chapel was dedicated to the Holy Saviour. (See No. 60.)

[9] '*kneeling down*,' &c. The position of the officiating minister at the Communion
table was then, as now, a subject of controversy. The next year (1635) Archbishop
Laud, at a visitation, insisted on the Communion table being placed altarwise, but
John Williams, bishop of Lincoln, denounced this as an innovation.

[10] '*Parr fold*,' on the road between Ringley and Stoneclough.

home and all the rest returned and howsoever good ould Elisha
was content to give us his trouble and fees which he telleth us is
10*l*., yet his men like so many Gehazis keepe a Racket that I
verily think it will cost us one way and other 5 marks before it
be finished.

Concerning your letter[11] to the Bishop I think it was both full
of pyete and policie and I know not how you could have written
better for your Denyall to disclose what you would doe per-
swaded the ould Craftie BB that indeed you would doe nothing
whilst you lived for so I heard him say and therefore he being so
far engaged in the action alreadie by the acceptance of our tender
of the 100*l*. was glad to Consecrate the Chapel with 10*l*. Dowrie,
who before stood upon 20 markes for he thought we could secure
no more, and Indeed to speak the truth I have for that 10*l*. pr
Ann. morgaged almost all that little I have and thank God for
so much, but now that it is made a Chapel, whatsoever is I intended for it above that 10*l*. may be of course taken with and
disposed of according to your mind. I could desire that you
would come down as soone as well you could or els I must come
up to you it will be better than writing and reading these long
scroles ; the Green Hall is yet unsould and if it were not at more
money than it is worth it would fitt well for it is a very dear purchas, but I think we cannot buy it for 13 score pounds —

My advice is if you give Lo. BB. anie thanks let it be verbal
not real but speare your money for better purposes and do not
grass[12] a fat sow behind so I rest

Yours

Pilkington this   PETER SEDDON.
    14 December 1634.

Yet my Lo. hath promised that whilst he and you Live whom
you name shall be the man for Minister.

---

[11] '*your letter.*' (See No. 22 and note.)
[12] '*grass,*' &c., *i.e., grease.* Peter is quoting a Lancashire proverb.

XXV.—*Addressed To my very loving frend Peter Seddon
in the Owtwood of Pilkington.*

Neighbour Peter,

I had apoynted you to have rec[d] that 8*l.* of Jo: Marsh, but he
hath brought it hither therefore because of my promisse I have
sent it backe agayne, call to him for it, and I will pay my self
when it comes, for it is not come yet, M[r] Win[13] will come from
Lancaster Assyzes to Pilkington and I have desyred his Assist-
ance to right me Agaynst those two unchristianlyke Teñants
Crompton[14] and Bassen, that have my house and gardens and
will pay no rent, he hath willed me to wryte to Mr Tho: fox[15] to
put hym in mynd of what I would have done, and he will doe it,
and I desyre your helpinge hand when it comes in question, for
I trobled Mr Langley[16] and you, first of all, and you have not
yet forgotten some passages, that base ill naturde Comptō, when
my Cosin Wilson[17] demanded ye rent, told him, (for ought he
knew) he had as much right to it as I ; whereas he confessed to
you at first as by your lře apeares, that Stable, Chamber, garden
and backe syde, he held of me, and further confessed he payd
but 24*s.* per añ:, but Jo: Bradsh: and all ye neighbours said he
payd 30*s.*, and now ye gentleman is not Ashamed to Chalenge it
for his owne, I have beene with my Lo: Strange about it, and he
hath given orders to Mr Win, to call him in questiō for his lease,

---

[13] '*Mr Win.*' Roger Wingate was the lawyer through whom Nathan bought his
estate at Benton in Yorkshire. He had a house near Hull, where Nathan Walworth
visited him in August 1639. See Nos. 50 and 55.

[14] '*Crompton.*' A "John Crompton of Pilkington" was tenant of property in
Manchester, owned by Raphe Seddon, in 1607. See No. 66.

[15] '*fox.*' See No. 6 and note.

[16] '*Mr Langley.*' Perhaps Mr. William Langley, the minister at Edenfield and
Holcomb, who was afterwards silenced by the second Lancashire 'classis.'

[17] '*Cosin Wilson.*' William, son of James Wilson of Poppythorn, in Prestwich,
married there (February 1624), Hester, daughter of Peter Walworth of Ringley, and
niece of Nathan Walworth. He died in his father's lifetime (see No. 53); and in his
Will, dated July 1640, named as overseer, his brother-in-law, Nathan Walworth
("cosin Nathan"). The Wilson family, for many generations, occupied Poppythorn,
which is part of the glebe of the rectory of Prestwich (see Booker's *Prestwich*).

and Bassen for his, and then we shall see how they Incroach and
wronge me, and I by reason of sufferinge them so longe, and my
Cosin Nathans connivence, have brought my piggs to a fayre
markett, but I will wryte my mynd fullye to M^r fox, agaynst M^r
Wins cominge, I am sory to be so troblesome to my frends but
I cannot help it, for my Lo^{ds} officers come at such a tyme as I
can not possibly come my self but must desyre the help of others,
and I will be as readye to help them in any thinge that lyes in
me, and so with comendations to your self, and your wyfe, I end
with my paper,   Yours

NATH: WALWORTHE.

Mar: 18
  1635.

————

XXVI.—*Addressed To my very loving frend Peter Seddon
in the Owtwood of Pilkington.*

Neighbour Peter[18]

you have beene put to a great deale of troble in Answeringe
so punctuallye to the particular hinderances of obtayninge this
Act, wch I can answer in one word without all this labour, the
true lett[19] is, your strayt fist, no peny, no pater noster, let the
B:^{pp} have his fees, and let his Clerkes have their fees, I will see
all payd, and let Mr Dercye[20] know he shall be well payd, and I
warrant you it will not be so difficult a matter to be done, and
Comend me to him, and let me have no more delayes, with ifs,
and ands, this, and that, for nothinge will Satisfye me but the
thinge it self, as my Councell tells me, and if you had beene but
as wyse as a goose, you might have done it, longe since. you
are in the same case about your minister for you will part with

---

[18] This letter is not dated, but comes in here as Bishop Bridgeman signed the
Sentence of Consecration ("this Act") on 1 June 1635.

[19] *'the true lett,' i.e., hindrance.* Cf. Shakespeare, "my speech entreats that I may
know the let, why gentle peace should not expel these inconveniences" (*Hen. V.*,
act v, sc. 2).

[20] *'Mr. Dercye.'* The Bishop's Registrar. See next letter.

nothinge, and yet you thinke to have a minister, get one for
shame, and lett him know from me, I will make his meanes,
worth 20*l.* a yeare at the least, keepe this lr̄e, and let my hand
witnes agaynst me, if I performe it not, I sent you a Copye of
an Accquittance, wch I bad you keepe off 20*s.* by will from M^r
Nevet, to be payd every May day for ever to the minister of
Ringley Chappell, if you have never a minister, lett any one that
supplies ye place for ye tyme, send his accquittance, and I will
call for it at the Girdlers Hall[21] and thus w^t comendations to
your self and your wyfe, I committ you to god and rest

Your Assured lovinge frend

NATHAN WALWORTHE.

I had forgotten one thinge, you talke of priviledges for y^e
Chappell and this and that, speake not of them, by any meanes,
till somethinge be done,

XXVII.—*Addressed To my very loving frend Peter Seddon
in the Owtwood of Pilkington.*

Neighbour Peter, I begin now to be a little more Calme, and
not so Angry as I was, my Stomacke is come Downe, heere I
send a letter to the BB: as you willed in the behalf of Mr. Hilton,[22]

---

[21] '*Girdlers Hall*' in Basinghall Street. This company was incorporated by
Hen. VI. in 1449. In 1568 the Pinners and Wire-pullers were united with the
Girdlers. Their crest is a "demy-effigy" of St. Lawrence, holding in the right hand
a grid-iron, in the left a book. Their motto is, "Give thanks to God." Maitland,
writing about a century ago, describes the hall as "well wainscotted within and containing a beautiful screen."

[22] '*Mr. Hilton.*' His real name was "William Hulton," and he so signs himself
in a list of householders living at Ringley in 1641. But so careless were our ancestors
about spelling that we find this entry in the *Manchester Court Leet Records*, "John
Hultonn died Oct 1583 ; son and heir Randle *Hilton.*" The bishop kept his promise
and appointed Mr. Hulton minister, for "Maister Hulton now minister at Ringley"
is mentioned as a legatee in the will of William Hulme, date 20 December 1637.
Mr. Hulton was probably ejected by the Presbyterians, in or before the year 1647,
when Mr. Holland "received a call" to Ringley, for in February 1652, the Bury
"classis" complained of Mr. Hulton for taking upon himself to "exercise in public"

and goe you to William Lever,[23] Robert Levers brother, and he will pay you the five markes,[24] and the 20s., but I must desyre to have a bill or note how, or for what it is payd, and that I hope is but reason, I am more trobled now, and have more busines then I have had this 20 yeare, and yet it shall goe hard, but I will make a steppe before Bartlemewtyde to see what a Coyle you keepe,[25] let there be no more cheese wantinge ; nor men to be kilde at Goffs,[26] and comend me to your wyfe, and I will be,

Your lovinge frend

Bay: Castle   NATHAN WALWORTHE
June, 12, 1635.

Mr. Walworth

The fees due by our table for the consecrating of a chappell is twentie nobles [27] whereof I have received five markes

THO: DARCY.

XXVIII.— *Addressed To my lovinge frend Peter Seddon in the Owtwood*

Neighbour Peter, you thinke it longe perhaps, that I send not the lre of Attorney, I have stayd all this whyle for Mr Urme-

and for baptising children, as they doubted if such baptisms were not null and void, he being a man "very insufficient and unworthy." Mr. Hulton was the eldest son of George Hulton of Farnworth and Margaret, daughter of Robert Hyde of Hyde and Norbury, and was baptised at Bolton in July 1594. In February 1624 he married, at Prestwich, Dorothy, the elder daughter of Raphe Seddon of Prestolee and sister of "neighbour" Peter, by whom he had several children.

[23] '*Wm. Lever*' of Kersal, the youngest brother of James Lever of Darcy Lever. He married Elizabeth, daughter of George Kenyon of Kersal, and died in 1646. For Robert Lever, see No. 16 and note.

[24] '*five marks*,' i.e., 3l. 6s. 8d. (See No. 24.) Ecclesiastical fees were fixed by John Whitgift, archbishop of Canterbury, in 1597. Cf. The Canons Ecclesiastical of 1603, No. cxxxv. [J. E. B.]

[25] '*what a coyle you keepe*,' i.e., "what you are doing"; *coil* means 'bustle,' 'stir.' Cf. "They talk of this and that, and keep a coyl and a pother about it." (Shadwell's *True Widow*, 1679.) "Well, well, said Blount, here is a coil about a cloak." (Scott's *Kenilworth*, chap. xv.)

[26] '*at Goff's*,' i.e., at Goffe's house. (See No. 29.)

[27] '*twenty nobles*'= 6l. 13s. 4d.

stones cominge[28] to y[e] towne, and I have spoken to him, and he hath not yet done it, but what matter is it, unlesse you had some thinge ready whereupon to lay it, you need it not unlesse you will put it in some bodyes hands to Improve it, I will draw it my self and send it tyme Inough ; we dranke your 12[d] merilye and who thinke you was at the Drinkinge of it but M[ris] Margret fox,[29] alias M[ris] Hyne, my old scoole fellow, whom I have not seene these 47 yeares, hir mother was my god mother, and she is now as lyke hir, as she can looke, and so w[t] comendations to your self and your wyfe I committ you to god and rest

Your lovinge frend

Bay: Castle   NATHAN WALWORTHE
    Oct: 12, 1635

XXIX.—*Addressed To my lovinge frend Peter Seddon in the Owtwood of Pilkington*

Neighbour Peter, I had Answered your lre sooner but that the contents of it was answered in M[r] Hiltons[30] lre whereof I know he would acquaint you and I had not written now but onelye to condole my disaster, I studied longe, and tooke a great deale of

----

[28] '*Mr. Urmeston.*' Probably Richard Urmeston of Westlegh, in the county of Lancaster. In 1641 the Urmestons got into trouble for refusing to sign the protestation, and, apparently, for 'harbouring priests.' Richard Urmeston was arrested, and orders were given "to search his trunk at Mr. Elton's chambers in the Inner Temple." Mr. Urmeston was soon afterwards released on taking the oaths of allegiance and supremacy. [From a note by Mr. Bailey.]

[29] '*Mris. Margret fox*,' youngest daughter of Wm. Foxe of the Rhodes, and therefore "neighbour" Peter's aunt. She married Wm. Hinde, Fellow of Queen's College, Oxford ; chaplain to James earl of Derby and vicar of Bunbury, in the county of Chester. Mr. Bruen of Stapleford, who married her sister Anne, mentions his sister-in-law Mrs. Hinde and her brothers William and Thomas Foxe, who joined him in the evenings when "my mother-in-law giving me table for a year, we set up the exercise of religion in the house." Mr. Hinde mentions Nathan's god-mother as "a godly matron descendant of the ancient families of Adderton and Leland," and Canon Raines is hence able to identify her as Margaret daughter of Henry Orrell of Orrell. (See Hinde's *Life of Bruen*.)

[30] '*Mr. Hilton*,' i.e., William Hulton the new minister at Ringley.

paynes, to Indyte a lr̄e of Attorney, wch I had done longe agoe,
and thought to send it now, and now I have sought 2 dayes and
2 nights for it, and cannot fynd it, I have quyt lost it and if you
would give me 100*l.*, I cannot wryte such an other, I followed
not your way, I could not abyde to have my name so often
named in it but onelye, Whereas there is a Chappell built by one
(not naming who) and y^r neighbourhood have promissed to give
towards &c: but it is not a poynt matter whether I make a lr̄e
of Attorney or no, you may collect it without it, and I could
wish it were collected and put out for ye benefyte of the Chapell,
or Scoole, and if you cannot gett it without such a lr̄e from me,
then let Goffe a Sharpons[31] and my Cousins ma that durst not
cry lest ye beast[32] put hir hornes in to his mouth, and such other
as are wyse and learned frame an other, by knockinge their
heads together and I will signe it, and so god send you a mery
Christmas, I am,

Your true, honest frend

Bay: Castle   NATHAN WALWORTH
   Dec: 12, 1635

———

XXX. — *Addressed To my lovinge neighbour Peter Seddon
in the Owtwood*

Neighbour Peter,

your lr̄e consists of 3 parts, quar̄u prima, is of the out Ile[33]
of the Scoole, whereof never aske me any question, but advyse

---

[31] '*Goffe a Sharpons*,' as we should say Geoffrey Sharples, but originally no doubt
Geoffry of Sharples, a village two miles from Bolton on the road to Darwen. Cf. the
name of Dick a Barlow (No. 36) from Barlow, near Manchester, and the name still in
use of a Becket from Becket, near Farringdon, in the county of Berks. Michael Drayton
sings :

    " Of Scarlock, *George a Green* and Much the miller's son
      Of Tuck the merry friar, which many a sermon made
        In praise of Robin Hood, his outlaws and their trade."

[32] '*ye beast*.' See No. 1.

[33] '*out Ile*.' Nathan uses this word again (No. 41) in the sense of "outhouse."
Perhaps it should be written "out-aisle," from the French, "aile," a wing, as we
speak of the "aisle" of a church.

with the best workmen you can gett and make it as hansome as
you can, and spare for no Cost so it be well ; and let the maisters
Chamber be trimbt up fitlye, and convenientlye you have laid
out 5*l*. and upward, I have given order to my Cosin wilson to
pay you the 5*l*., and when ye rest is done I will pay you all

Secunda, is about Babilayes,³⁴ I have not my lease of Babilayes yet ; but when I have it, what hopes have you ? or what
encouragement can you give me ? wherby I may be drawne to
beleeve, it will be a fitt thinge for that purpose, and so remayne
for ever, wch when I know, I will give you myne Answere,

Pertia, is about a coate or somewhat for Goffe a Sharples (for,
as for ye other thinge about ye letter I say nothinge of it, as
being unworthy the answering) but I will not so passe over Goffe,
but he shall heare from me shortlye,

and now I have somewhat to say to you, how chanceth it that
Mr Hilton³⁵ wrytes to me, to help him to his money, what a
shame is it for you all ? that, after all that I have done, I must
yet be troubled with these things, especiallye consideringe I have
given 20*s*. to pay the charges of them that gather it, shall I never
be quyet ? I confesse I take it ill, and it was undeservedlye done
of him to wryte to me : for what have I to doe with it now ?
but it may be you have compelled him, let it be what it will,
it is naught ; I say no more,

                                   Yours, NATH: WALWORTHE.
Bay: Castle
    feb: 13, 1636.

XXXI. — *Addressed To my very loving frend Peter Seddon
        in the Owtwood in Pilkington.*

Neighbour Peter,

Your woman³⁶ is come safe to Londō I have been w^t my Lo:
Strange, and have shewed Mr Wiñ all my deeds and he hath

---

³⁴ '*Babilayes.*' In his Will Nathan leaves his estate, for three lives, called Babiles
at Brockenbanke (probably in Broughton) to his Nephew, Nathan the younger.
³⁵ '*Mr. Hilton.*' See No. **27**, and note.

taken a note of them, and my Lo: hath given him directions
what to doe, I am afrayd he will be gone before this lr̄e come to
your hands, stand to me now as you will ever have me to sticke
to you and doe but deale wysely with Comptō, and you shall
gett those that will prove he payd 30s. per ann̄, as Jo: Bradsh:
and others, and if you can but prove that once, lett me alone
with him, and so lykewyse for Bassen, you know she had but 30
foote from the street backward, but I must be gone, I was never
so full of busines in all my lyfe send me my lr̄e safe agayne,
farewell,

N: WALW:

Apr: 7.
1636

XXXII.—*Addressed To my very loving frend Peter Seddon
in the Owtwood of Pilkington.*

Neighbour Peter,

I have rec^d your packett, but you fayle in one thinge as wyse
as you are, I suppose you have rec^d of Jo: Marsh the 8l. for
Mr Hilton, and why then doe not you acknowledge so much? for
Crompton, I care not a fart for him, the gardens are free land,
and the houses Indeed are my Lords,[37] but I have answered that
to Mr Wiñ, I shall longe to heare what is done,

I have made fortye Iorneys to Whytehall for Elin but can doe
no good, the sicknes[38] begins in London and the ki: will suffer

---

[36] '*your woman*,' *i.e.*, Peter's wife, Ellen Seddon, mentioned in the next letter.
She had come to London, hoping to be touched by king Charles for king's evil.
(Sext next letter and note.)

[37] '*My Lord*,' *i.e.*, Lord Strange, for William earl of Derby, though still alive, had
resigned his Lancashire estates to his son, and lived in retirement at Chester, where he
died September 1642.

[38] '*the sickness*,' *i.e.*, the plague, then very prevalent in England. Dr. Worthington
writes on January 8 1636-7, "began the University sermons in St. Mary's, which, by
reason of the plague, were prohibited from the beginning of November." (*Worthington's
Diary*, edited by James Crossley, Esq.)

G

no diseased persons to come neere him,[39] yet there were some
healed, but it was such as had some noble mans letter, and it was
done privatelye in the garden, all the rest are sent away and
apoynted to come agayne at Mich: if the sicknes cease you sent
6ᵈ by hir to drinke, and I warrant you we have bought no land
with it ; and so I end with 1000 commendations, restinge,

                         Your assured frend
                                NATHAN WALWORTHE.

Bay: Castle
   Apr: 21, 1636.

[39] '*The king*,' &c.   This refers to "touching" for the king's evil or scrofula.
From the time of Edward the Confessor to that of George I. a power of healing was
claimed by the sovereign of England.   The kings of France also "touched" for scrofula,
for Servetus, writing in 1535, says, "I have myself seen the king (Francis I.) touching
many labouring under the disease, but I did not see that they were cured."   James I.
was not supposed to possess this royal virtue when king of Scotland, but the power
is said to have come to him immediately after his accession to the English throne,
and much bloodshed might have been avoided, if this test had been applied to the
many claimants for our throne from "the Conqueror" to "the Pretender."   The
Form of Healing occurs often in the Common Prayer Books of the reign of Charles I.,
Charles II., James II. and Queen Anne.

   A Latin form was used in the time of Henry VII., and it was reprinted in 1686
by the king's printer.   On Good Friday 1639, King Charles "touched" 200 persons
at York, and while he touched the sick "were read these words, 'They shall lay their
hands upon the sick and they shall recover.'   While the king put about their necks
an angel of gold, were read these words, 'That light was the true light which lighteth
every man which cometh into the world.'"   (Drake's *Eboracum*, p. 137.)

   From registers duly kept, we learn that from 1660 to 1682, as many as 92,107
persons were touched.   In 1683, a proclamation, published in every parish, fixed the
time for presenting persons for the "public healings."   George I. made no pretensions
to the miraculous gift, and it has never been claimed by his successors.   In connection
with this subject it is interesting to note that the native correspondent of a Yeddo
Journal, who accompanied the Mikado on his first tour through Japan in the summer
of 1876, says, "the lower class of people carefully gathered up the earth, which had
been pressed by the foot of their Sovereign, believing it would cure some of their
ailments."   He adds, "it is not so very long ago, since a superstition of this sort was
prevalent among the ignorant in Europe."   (See *The Times*, August 9 1876.)

XXXIII. — *Addressed To my lovinge frend Peter Seddon in the Owtwoode.*

Neighbour Peter, Sure, you have beene at Gregories,[40] when you sent me this to Seale, what? are you out of your witts? will you have me to seale that which is none of myne owne? if he brings 23*l.*, I have promissed, he shall redeeme it, I will say no more till I come, farewell,

Yours, NA: WALWORTHE.

July, 13
1636.

———

XXXIV.—*Addressed To my very loving frend Peter Seddon in the Owtwood of Pilkington.*

Neighbour Peter, I had a great Iorney, after I parted with you,[41] before I came to London, when I came home I reckoned it and found that I had gone 552 myle wch seemed the longer, because I had no Company but was all alone, and besydes of 200 of these myles I knew not one foote of the way, my best . help was, I had a good horse, and nether fall nor any mischance by ye way, I pray you thank William Seddons wyfe[42] for y^e

---

[40] '*at Gregories.*' Probably Gregory kept an ale-house (see next letter and No. 52). Thomas Gregorie of Outwood " took the Protestation " in 1641.

[41] Nathan had paid a visit to Pilkington and spent a night in Chester on his return.

[42] '*William Seddon.*' William Seddon, M.A., of Magd. Coll., Cambridge, and vicar of Eastham, had just been appointed 'preacher' at St. Mary's, Chester. During the siege of Chester (1645) he lodged in Bishop Bridgeman's palace, and frequently exhorted and encouraged the garrison, with whom he and his wife must have been popular, if they were always as hospitable as Nathan here intimates. After the surrender he was imprisoned, and his house plundered, and he applied for shelter to his brother Peter, then "turned zealous Presbyterian," who is said to have replied that "would he conform himself to ye Godly party his own merits would protect and prefer him." However, he found a friend in Mr. Atherton, who got him the rectory of Grappenhall, near Warrington. Again expelled by the Presbyterians, he acted as chaplain to John Fleetwood of Penwortham till the Restoration, when he returned to Grappenhall and died there (1671), aged 67. He was buried with his wife, who died the same month, in the chancel of his church. See No. 59.

[bottle] of green ginger she gave me, it refreshed me many tymes, when a quame, came over my stomacke I am now in my old closett in Bay: Castle, and not so much afrayd as I was many tymes by ye way though the sicknes be hott, and especially in our parish,[43] where there dyes weekely 7, 8, 9, or 10 of ye sicknes, and in all, through the whole citie 1400 and odd everye weeke, I delivered your letter at Chester, and your brother was at me betymes the next morninge, and what betweene burnt Ale, and then the Taverne, and then stronge beere agayne, one house after an other, it cost him soundly, he might have seene the Beares and the Lyons[44] better cheape,

I had no money when I was in Lanc: els I would have payd that bill for the Scoole, but dispatch you that wch is to be done and I will pay all, I sent the gold you lent me backe agayne by Tho: Parr frō Manchester, I pray you send me that lrē touchinge Crompton, if there be anythinge in it that you would remember, take a Copye of it before you send it, and thus w^t comendations and thanks to your self, and your wyfe, to Rob: Seddon and his soñs Rich: Hewood[45] your unckle Mihill, Goffe and Gregory I committ you to god and rest

Your assured loving frend

Bay: Castle   NATHAN WALWORTHE.
    Oct: 9, 1636.

---

[43] '*in our parish.*' The burial register of St. Bennet's, close to Baynard's Castle, shows that the mortality from the plague was fearful about this time.

[44] '*the Beares and the Lyons.*' I take this to mean that Nathan proposes, in jest, to repay the parson's hospitality, in an economical way, by taking him to see the Beargarden when he next visited London. The Bear-garden in Southwark existed from a very early date. The Tudors and Stuarts enjoyed the sport of bear-baiting, and generally introduced a new ambassador to the bear-garden as soon as his first audience was over. Here Master Slender saw "Sackerson," the famous bear (see the *Merry Wives of Windsor*); and Pepys often mentions his visits to the bears. Lions were to be seen in the Tower, where they were kept from the time of Hen. III. to that of William IV. They were named after the reigning kings, and there was a superstition, that when a king died the lion of that name died soon after him.

[45] '*Rich: Hewood*' of Little Lever, the father of Oliver and Nathaniel Heywood, the ejected ministers. In Oliver Heywood's *Life* he is mentioned as "a man of talent

XXXV.—*Addressed To my lovinge frend, Peter Seddon in the Owtwood of Pilkington.*

Neighbour Peter,

I have rec^d your lr̄e, but blame me not because I have not answered it sooner, they that give me cause of discontent, or backebyte, slander or calumniate me, god forgive them, the Divell is an Accuser and I hold them no better then Divells that accuse me of any Intent to wrong those orphans,[46] whom I am bound in a double bond to protect, no, I goe not about to wrong them, but to keepe off woolves y^t would añoy them, and when I made choyce of those so Indifferent (as I thought) feofees,[47] I thought I had eased my self of a great deale of care, and now their dissentions, Increaseth it, I have written to them what my Intent is, if they yeeld to me I will doe nothinge, but what I can Iustifye w^t a safe conscience, both before god and all the world, if not then I will trye my fortune, and because some things in the will may have a dooble meaninge, and are doubtfull, I thinke I shall be driven to send processe for you, and Robte Seddō to declare your mynds touchinge the same, seeinge I am put to it I will cleare my self as well as I may, Lord, what have I done? I have lived in a place of charge these (almost) 48 yeares,[48] and was never accused of any Iniustice or wronge done to any, and should I now begin? and upō Inocents? and myne owne kindred? I have done, my hand shakes I can wryte no more, and yet I am full, my belly will burst, when I sett my hand to that feoffment, my meaninge was, not so to exclude my self, as not

and enterprise and eminently religious." He was second cousin to 'neighbour' Peter, through his grandmother, the daughter of Peter Seddon of Prestolee, who died in 1575. In 1641-2, Richard Heywood, then residing at Whitefield in Pilkington, "took the Protestation." He died March 1st, 1677, aged 81, and was buried at Bolton.

[46] '*those orphans*,' *i.e.*, the two infant daughters of Ellis Walworth, who died in 1630, and appointed Nathan trustee of his children. (See No. 24, note 5.)

[47] '*indifferent feoffees*,' *i.e.*, impartial. Cf. Ecclus, xlii, 5. Dr. Johnson quotes Ascham "Medcalfe was partial to none, indifferent to all," and condemns the use of "indifferent" in the sense of "mediocre" as improper and colloquial.

[48] '48 years,' in other words, ever since he was 17.

to have a voyce in the reconcylings of businesses, or if they were
all dead and I livinge, I might not have power to elect new feofees, if Robt Seddō might happelye leave out such a proviso
what then ? shall any man thereupon take the advantage, to
wronge me and the children, for it shall appeare when it comes
in question who it is that goes about to wronge the children, I
or they all my ayme is (howsoever I am traduced to yᵉ contrary)
to have the livings put out for the Childrens best advantage, and
I know it is a usuall thinge, you need not to bringe in, nor tell
me of Prestwich, Yate,[49] and others, I looke not that the Children
should plow, Sowe, sett or thresh, I have more care of them then
so ; but what need I to repeate a thinge so often, I will troble
you no further, but pray you (if it be not done already) to finish
all things about the Scoole, and I will see all discharged, when I
know what it comes to, and thus with my commendations to
your self and your wyfe, and to your brother,[50] when you wryte
commende me unto him and thanke him, and so desyringe your
prayers, I commit you to god, and rest

Your assured frend

Bay : Castle   NATHAN WALWORTHE.
    Novē: 25 1636.

XXXVI.—*Addressed To my very lovinge frend Peter
Seddon in the Owtwood of Pilkington.*

Neighbour Peter, I have now sent that wᶜʰ I promissed, I pray
you, harken after it,[51] there be two cases, and they will be left
with Mr. Rich: Lomas,[52] the cariage is payd, and they will be in
Manchester by Wensday noone at the furthest, you must send

---

[49] '*Yate.*'   Peter's sister-in-law, Anne Seddon, married a Yate.

[50] '*your brother,*' *i.e.*, William Seddon.   (See preceding letter.)

[51] '*harken after it.*'   Nathan elsewhere writes, "you had harkened after Greenhall"
(No. 39), and "why do you not harken out something" (No. 40).   Cf. Shakespeare,
"He harkens after prophecies and dreams" (*Richard III.*, act i, sc. 1.)

[52] '*Rich: Lomas.*'   See No. 23 and note.

your cart for them and I will pay you, be carefull in caryinge
them, you may either sett them edglinge or flatt with the
chalkye syde upward, let Dick a Barlow sett them up and see
there be no help wantinge, for feare of Breakinge any thinge, I
hope all will come safelye I have taken all the care I could in
the packinge, if you goe not for them till thursday morninge,
you may give Dick a Barlow[53] warning, and let him come with
you as you come backe, and unpacke them presentlye and sett
them up, this inclosed note will direct you, I shall longe till I
heare how all is dispatched, therefore make hast and let me heare
by the first, and in so doinge, you shall oblige

Your poore frend

Bay: Castle   NATHAN WALWORTHE.
June, 6. 1637.

XXXVII.— *Addressed — Mr. Walworths Instructiō touching
touching the armes.*

May. 16,
    1637.

Directions to open the Cases.

first observe that, that syde wch is chalked is the upper syde—
ripp open the boards upō that syde—

be carefull in takinge off the Crowne wch is fastened w^t 3
nayles, and a coard in the end—the lower syde board is fastened
with 5 or 6 nayles to the lower part of the Armes wch must be
carefully ript off w^t a thin chisell—the unicornes horne lyes
wrapped in a paper at the backe of the unicorne—

there be 2 plates of Iron fastened to ye bottom of the Armes,
to nayle them fast to the skreene—care must be taken to sett

---

[53] '*Dick a Barlow.*' Richard Barlow of Pilkington, summoned as a witness against
Isaac Allen in 1645. Apparently he was hard to please, for two years later (1647)
he complained to the Presbyterian Assembly, that he and his mother were forbidden
by Toby Furness, the incumbent of Prestwich, to come to communion "because they
were short in their answers at ye eldership, and there was no objection of scandal
against them." (See Booker's *Prestwich.*)

the Armes Just in the middle, and the 2 lesser Armes[54] at the 2 ends in an equall proportion, Derby house, before the other,—

but the greatest care of all that no help be wantinge whereby in the liftinge them up, for want of help any thinge be broken, brused, or disfigured—

the smaller Armes have 3 Iron pins, wch are to be lett in with an half Inch auger—

the boards of the cases, let them serve to pay the Charges of setting up the Armes—

XXXVIII. — *Addressed To my very loving frend Peter Seddon in the Owtwood of Pilkington.*

Neighbour Peter,

I marvyle not a little, that you are so backward and slacke in gatheringe in this money wch might have beene (ere this) Imployed to the benefyte of the Scoole you know what you promissed and the rest of ye Neighbourhood at the Beginninge, and not onelye promissed, but past it under hand and Seale, to pay vl. when any thinge was found out, and assured for the mayntenance of a minister you also know, that there is a Stipendiary maintenance for a minister, w^ch, (though not so larg as I could wish) yet, competent, and assured, and I would all the Chappells in Engl: were no worse provyded for, and yet notwithstandinge, you for your parts have not performed your promis nor in any wyse done, as men that stand either upon honestye, Credit, or Conscience, (I am sory to speake it) but what would you have me to say? you are lyke unto those that St. Bern: speakes of qui omnem velint sine sumptu excersere [55] pietatem, you will serve god of free cost, but rather then be at any charges you will for sake god, religiō and all, thus the Divell accused Job : that he served god for his owne gayne, Job : 1, 9. but he was (lyke

---

[54] '2 *lesser Armes*,' *i.e.*, those of Derby and Pembroke, which, in the new church, are placed over the north porch door.

[55] '*excersere*' *i.e.*, exercere.

him self) a lyer, the prophet David, could say, I will not offer a
sacrifise of that which cost me nothinge 2 Sam: 24, 24 ; I wonder
what we would have done if we had lived in those tymes under
the Law when the service of god was more chargeable than it is
now ; I thinke we would have offered but leane sacrifyces ; when
we stumble at so small a thinge as this, especiallye when after
the payment heereof you are freed for ever after ; I could say
much more, if I were amonge you face to face, but I have not
tyme to wryte at large, but I heare there are some amonge you,
that thinke they are freed frō paying their money because (say
they) I forgave them, butt my meaninge was not so ; but thus it
was, I was sory to see the Chappell so long unprovyded of
meanes, and I saw you were slow Inough, for although you had
harkened after Greene Hall, and an other place or two, yet
nothinge was brought to passe, nor came to perfection, and it
greeved me to heare everye body say O it is pittie great pittie,
there is not meanes for the Chappell and so every body stood as
over a man in a ditch, every one sayd it is pittye he should lye
there, but no man would put to his hand to help him out, then I
endevoured to see what I could doe, and (to be short) I did that
wch you see, and because it was farr above your abilitie to com-
pass it, I meant to bestow 200*l*. and you the other 200*l*., and to
that end we had a meetinge at ye Chappell and there I proposed
it, and when I saw you were such Gadarens such Demases and
such earthewormes, that you would not streatch your selves to
doe any more then Iust what you had promissed under hand
and seale to doe, then I refused to Ioyne with you in the purchase, but absolutely away let it goe ; although it was, both
above my power, and meaninge too, for either you should be at
ye charge of the one half, or none at all with me, but that w^{ch}
you would doe, you should doe, and that wch I would doe, I
would doe, and I have done my part, now doe you yours, and
because you thinke the Chappell sufficiently endowede, (but I
thinke not so) you may convert it to a Scoole wch will be as
good, but (for very shame) doe some thinge, y^t may be a memory

to posteritie, and may be an encouragement to your succeedinge
generations to follow your good exãple and thanke god that you
are no more burdened, for if that were not done wch is done you
could not have avoyded it but ye B:PP of ye Dioces, would have
compelled you to have mentayned a minister, frō yeare to yeare,
and frō age to age for ever, wch would have beene a greater
charge, I blame not all, not those that are willinge, and unable,
but those that are able, and unwillinge, I must end with my
paper

                              NATHAN WALWORTHE.
July, 3, 1637.

                    ———

XXXIX.—*Addressed To my very loving frend Peter Seddon
          in the Owtwood of Pilkington.*

Neighbour Peter

I had made ready my bill of complaynt[56] with Birches
Answere, and all other things, to have sent them to you, and to
the Arbitrators,[57] and now all is Dasht ; Martha hath written
unto me, intreatinge me to wryte my mynd, but to what end ?
for if I should wryte my mynde who would follow it ? no,
it is to no end, all must rest as it is, till I can have tyme to
come my self, thus much in Answere of your last, I cannot en-
large my self as I would, my Lā: is come hither and I am driven
to make provision for all thinges, I have scarce any tyme to
pisse, or els I had answered your former long lr̃e before this, w^ch
though I cannot have tyme fullye to answere yet some thing I
will say, the first part of your lr̃e whollye concernes the busines
in Ringley to wch I shall need to say no more then I have said
already, the second is onelye of Jo: Holme,[58] with whom I hope
you are able to deale well Inough seeing the case is playne,

---

[56] '*bill of complaynt*.' A bill in Equity to compel specific performance of the con-
tract entered into to subscribe towards the chapel endowment. [R. S. S.]

[57] '*the Arbitrators*.' Probably Mr. Allen and Mr. Serjeant (see No. 44). *Martha*,
Ellis Walworth's widow, mentioned in No. 24.

[58] '*Jo: Holme*.' See No. 47, and note.

the third is to bring the Chappell and Scoole to unitie, to wch I say, you know I have but 53*l.* 4*s.*, and 28*l.*, 20*l.* more is to come in about Mar: and Holme and doodson 10*l.*, all wch will make not above 111*l.* and odd, and what I pray you will y^t purchase? my drift was to gett it together, and put it out to Improve it, for ye better advancing the Scoolem^{rs} meanes, now if you take that Improvement for the mayntenance of the Scoolem^r then ye store will never ryse higher then about 110*l.*, and 110*l.* will never pur-chase above 5 per annū for perpetuitie, wch is but a poore thinge, therefore lett it goe as it doth, and I will give 5*l.* per anñ to ye scoolem^r till somethinge be purchassed, and it shall begin, frō this last Christmas, if you all consent heercunto, call to my Cosin Wilson, and he shall pay you 5*l.*, if not, I will send you what hath beene made, and doe with it what you will, and you may keepe that wch will come in now at Candlemas too, but when all this is done, will 5*l.* or theereabouts mayntaine a scoolem^r so that the contributors, and those that have payd their 5*l.* shall send their children to scoole and be free from any further charge? I trow not, what then is to be done? consider of all these things, and tell me what you will have me to doe and I will doe it, I should answere the m^{rs} lrē,[59] but you see tyme will not give me leave, and this lrē partly answers his, doe as well as you can till I come, wch I will endevour to doe as soone as I can, and in the meane tyme you see my meaninge, wherein if I err I will submitt myself to better Iudgments and rest as ever

Yours, NATH: WALWORTHE.

Jan: 25 1638.

XL.—*Addressed To my very lovinge frend Peter Seddon in the Owtwood of Pilkington.*

Neighbour Peter,

I know ere this, you have rec^d Answere to all the particulars of this your last lrē dated Ja: 29, you must not blame me if I doe

<hr/>

[59] '*mrs. lrē,*' *i.e.*, schoolmaster's letter.

not presentlye and at the Instante answere everye lr̄e that comes
from you, sometymes my busines will not give me leave, if you
would give me 10*l.* for a lr̄e, as now for example, my La: sent
worde to come hither presentlye after Christmas, and she came
w⁴in 3 dayes after twelftyde, I must have some tyme to prepare
the house, and if a lr̄e come to me in the midst of my busines ;
must I let all alone and answere your lr̄e? none of your lr̄es.
have miscaryed as you may see by my Answere both to you
and the Mʳˢ lr̄e, I am glad you have Doodsons 5*l.*, and some hope
of Robinsons, as for Holme, if he pay it to me I will receive it,
and be Accomptable for it but I feare he will never pay it unto
me, and for that money you have, and are to receive, I had rather
you keepe it then send it to me, so you put it into good mens
hands, for this is not an age, to let out money, and why doe not
you harken out somethinge to be purchassed as well as I but
put all upon my backe, this last 28*l.* is in my hands still, I dare
not put it out, the other 50*l.*, is abroad, god send it well in agayne,
we live in a madd age, for other matters, as I heare by your
Answere to my former lr̄e so I will consider and dispose, and
for the present trouble you no further but rest

                    Your constant frend
Bay Castle   NATHAN WALWORTHE.
  feb: 7, 1638.

After I had finished my lr̄e, lookinge over yours agayne I
found you Intimated that I should not preferr the yonger soñe
before yᵉ elder, and you Instance in old Isaake but therein you
are out, it was Iacob, Isaak Indeed blessed yᵉ yonger, but it was
unwillinglye, he was cosened by reason of decay of his sight, but
Iacob, as the text sayth directed his hand of purpose gen: 48.
14; for that when you aleadge Scripture to me you must be
wyser heereafter, least I take you nappinge, thus much by the
way, you shall not need to feare my doinge, for I doe Subscrybe
to your opinion, and am utterlye agaynst the Pride of ————
I say no more farewell

                              NATH WALWORTHE.

XLI.—*Addressed To my very lovinge frende Peter Seddon*
in ye Owtwood of Pilkington.

Neighbour Peter, it is the fashion of those that are guilty, ever
to cry (whore) first, I never rec^d any lrē from you since the 4 of
Sept and that was in ye behalf of Rich: Heape[60] about a matter
betweene Robinson and him and I Answered his lrē, and told
him also what you had written in his behalf and would have done
his busines but he writt to the Contrarye, and since then I never
hard word from you, it is not my manner but to give Answere to
a very kitchen boy, if he wryte unto me, but this is not all, I have
worse matter than this, if I were a man given to requyt evill for
evill, but (I thanke God) I am not, I gave my mā leave at Christmas to see his frends, and I sent tokens into Ringley and Kersley,
(Indeed I writt not to you, for I looked to have hard from you,
that all about the scoole had beene finished by that tyme) and
he and his unckle George Hardman[61] came to the Chappell, and
stayed the Sermon, and you did not so much as looke on them,
or aske how I did, or whether I was alyue or dead, or offer them
the common curtesye of ye Cuntry, wch I should have done to
any though he had come as farr as Barwick,[62] much more to any
y^t should come out of ye Owtwood or Prestwich parish; I know
your answere will be, you nether saw them nor knew them but is y^t
lykely? can strangers (especially Londoners) be at a Sermon in
the Chappell, and no notice taken of them?; but I spend too
much tyme upon so bad a Subiect, let me come to that wch is
more materiall you wryte (for newes) the mortalitie of dyvers
of your neighbours, and if that be true wch is written in ye epist:
to ye Heb: 9, 27: in Deu: 31, 14; Job: 14. 5: Ecc: 8, 8; 2 Sa: 14,
14; Eccl 14. 17; then I wonder not so much that they are dead,

---

[60] '*Heape.*' A contributor to the chapel fund.

[61] '*George Hardman.*' One of the witnesses to Nathan's Will.

[62] '*Barwick.*' Perhaps Barwick Basset, near Marlborough, in Wilts, where Lord
Pembroke may have had property; but the argument is obscure. Nathan either
means, "Had he only come a short distance from Barwick I would have shown him
courtesy much more," &c., or he means "Were he an utter stranger from the end of
England (Berwick-on-Tweed) I would have shown him courtesy much more," &c.

as that they have lived so longe, for (except Hoome[63]) they were all of those yeares that by the course of nature they must needs dye, and I thinke you take me to be a Nestor[64] or a Methusala, and that I shall never dye or els you would never have beene so longe in finishinge a poore scoole wch was not above 5 or 6 dayes worke, and I speake to you to dispatch it, that I might live to see it done, and this is 2 yeares the next Aug: since, and yet it is not done O that you served a Lady[65] that I served, you needed not to have carde where you had begde your bread, I am sure if I had served hir so I might have begde my bread, or els have come home and lyved of the Almes of the parishe, I have perused your bill, and it comes to 8*l*. 3*s*., this last Account, but there was a former Account when I gave you 10*l*., and then you rec^d of Will Seddō and Ro: Sedd: 5*s*. of Ric: Haywood[66] and Ellis farnworth Junior 5*s*. of Ell: farn: sen^r 6*d*. in all 10*s*. 6*d*., let this 10*s*. 6*d*., be restored agayne, to them that be living, or to the wyues of them that be dead I have payd it to Tho. Parr and sealed it up in this lrē as you may see by the Accompt, wherein I haue taken some paynes, thinkinge once to have an end, but it will never be, I must stay for an other account about a little out-ile, or hovell for wood or coles, wch I could have done my self in half a day and I must stay 2 yeares more for that,

I have not done Chydinge yet ; I know not where the fault is, nor who to blame, but is it not strange ? that the Chappell money can not be gathered in all this whyle, but one drawes one way and an other drawes an other way, one will have it for the Chappell, and an other will have it for the scoole, but the drift is

[63] '*Hoome*.' John Holme's brother. See No. 47.

[64] '*a Nestor*.' Nathan was then sixty-seven.

[65] '*a Lady*.' Anne, countess of Pembroke, who had (says Whitaker) "the courage and liberality of the other sex, with the devotion, order, and economy, *perhaps not all the softness*, of her own."

[66] '*Ric: Haywood*,' See No. 34, and note. *Ellis Farnworth, junior*, is perhaps alluded to in No. 1 ; his name appears in the list of contributors to Mr. Holland in 1652, when Ellis Farnworth, senior, was probably dead, as Widowe Farnworth is mentioned in the same list. See No. 64.

to keepe it, and not to part with it at all, I am ashamed and sory to have bestowed so much paynes and charges upon them that are so unworthy I am not sory nether doe I repent for the worke done, but that it is bestowed upon them that so little deserve it, I might have bestowed it in Wilshyre[67] where I was bredd, though not borne but my love to my Cuntry[68] made me myndfull of them, or I might have done it in London or about Londō where god hath blessed my endevours to make me able to doe it, but, "Nescio qua natale solū dulcedine" &c:[69] and thus am I requyted, that whereas they were yearely to maynetayne a minister wch is a continuall charge, now they are ridd of that, by the performinge of that wch they under their hands willingly promissed ; and now what a toyle is heere to get it,? I have stayd 2 yeares and cannot heare of any thinge that is done, and seeinge it is so, I will trust no more feofees but take the matter into my owne hands, and if I cannot get it, I will lose it, whatsoever therefore you have received alreadye, send it to me, I will be Accountable for it, and give me their names, what and how much everye one hath payd, as also of them y^t have not payd together with ye wrytinge and deede whereto their hands and scales are sett, and let me alone, and so I leave scoldinge,

for your busines (although you will not doe myne) yet I have done yours, and sent you such a payre of wayghts as all Lancash^r cannot sample nor match, you have sent 5s., and it is a good pryce, I could have sent you a payre for so much but I will never loose a hogge or sheepe for a penyworth of Tarr, I will never send a bad commoditie (for savinge a little money) and send a badd, these cost 6s. which is 12d. more then you sent, but this bearer hath payd it, and now I have done, and you may be glad,

---

[67] '*in Wilshyre*,' &c.   Probably in the house of his relative, Ralph Walworth, who had property in Salisbury.

[68] '*my Cuntry*,' *i.e.*, my county.   See No. 52, "commissioners in the country," where the word is used in the same sense.

[69] '*Nescio*,' &c.   Nescio quâ natale solum dulcedine cunctos

Ducit, et immemores non sinet esse sui.

Ovid. Pont., 1, 3, 35.

for as I have beene put to penance in wrytinge it, so you will lose
a dayes sowing of barlye (if all be not Sowne) or a dayes gettinge
of Turffs or weedinge corne, in readinge it, I could quyte[70] your
number of dead folkes, and treble it, if you knew them as well as
I knew those that you named, but I will onelye name one, wch I
thinke you knew and remember, Chivalier our french man who
dyed at Christmas last, but I have done (as I sayd) least I make
you as ill a husband[71] as my self, Vale, I am,

Yours

Bay: Castle   NATHAN WALWORTHE.
   Apr: 28, 1638

XLII.—*Addressed To my very loving frend Peter Seddon in
the Owtwood of Pilkington*

Neighbour Peter

Although at my first settinge forth I had Stormes of thunder
lighteninge, and rayne, yet after the first day the weather was
more Seasonable, and I performed my Iorney well and in good
tyme, I came up in 4 dayes[72] which was much for one that ridd
upō a trottinge dull Iade, I thanke god I am heere, and I must
also thanke you for my good entertainment ; as for the matter
in hand[73] I was content to put it to ye Arbitratiō of frends, but
you see there will be no end, for he shufiles from one thinge to
an other, now he denyes to goe off the one half, and claymes
it by the will, whereas he entered into band to goe off after two

---

[70] '*quyte*,' *i.e.*, quit, match.
[71] '*a husband*,' *i.e.*, a husbandman. So Dryden
" If continued rain
The lab'ring <i>husband</i> in his house restrain,"</div>
but perhaps the word means here, a *steward.* Cf.
" What ill husbands we are of so tender a fortune."
(Collier on Fame.)
[72] '*in 4 dayes.*' Nathan rode about 190 miles in the four days ; fair travelling for
a man of sixty-seven.
[73] '*the matter in hand*,' perhaps his "cosin's" Will. See No. 44.

yeares, there is no dealinge with a perverse and wranglinge
fellow, but, vi et armis, I pray you doe so much for me, as, let
your soñe[74] wryte it out, and send me the Copie of that will;
for myne is with my Counsell, and all my other wrytings, and I
can come by nothinge, and I would fayne see it, for my Satis-
factiō but let it be written verbatim, both for the tyme, and
witnesses and all, I hope by this tyme all yᵉ worke about Chapell
and Scoole is finished, take occasion to speake to Io: and Iam:
Ouldam[75] once more to see if that money will be payde without
further troble, and let me know, for I feare none but them two,
and thus with commendations to your self to your wyfe and
children, and the mayster, I end, I must away, for I am as thicke
in Daube and morter[76] heere as I was there farewell,

Your lovinge frend

Bay: Castle   NATHAN WALWORTHE
Aug: 16, 1638

————

XLIII.—*Addressed To my very lovinge frend Peter Seddon
in the Owtwood of Pilkington*

you make me wonder, alas, who does not know that the last
will must stand? and is not myne his last will? if this be not his
will, (havinge his owne hand to it, and witnesses, you and Roger
Dickson)[77] or a true copye of his last will, why did you send it
me, or if you know of an other will made afterward contrarye to
this, why told you me not sooner, but suffered me to be Abused
all this whyle, and to run at random and upō a false ground,
well, howsoever, I will see it, whatsoever it cost me, and when

———

[74] '*your son.*' Probably Neighbour Peter's eldest son Peter, who lived with his
father. See No. 57 and note.

[75] '*Io: and Ias: Oldham.*' They had not paid their contribution to the chapel
fund. See No. 59.

[76] '*Daube and morter,*' *i.e.,* plaster and mortar; daub is mortar without lime. In
Bucks the labourers call *lath and plaster, wattle and dab.*

[77] '*Roger Dickson*' mentioned in the next letter; he contributed to Mr. Holland
in 1652. See No. 64.

I

you saw Parr scrupelous and unwillinge, you should never have trobled M[r] Hilton nor Harry nor any body about it but let him keepe it, this denyinge and conccalinge it, gives suspition that there hath beene Iuglinge, for if there be difference, then that will is a will of their makinge and not of his, I pray you wryte your brother,[78] to get a copie of it, and whatsoever he layes out, let him send so much lesse when he sends his first fruits now at Alhollowtyde, and I will make it good, there will be no great search in fyndinge it he dyed about the beginninge of Decem: 1630 it is lykelye then the will was proved in the beginninge of 1631 I hope all is well about the Chappell and Scoole, and that I shall have no more troble, nor such bad Iorneys about them, I am sory for y[e] loose of your good Neighbour Robert Bolton,[79] there is one neerer y[e] Chappell, that might better have beene spared if it had so pleased god, sicknes is very sore and ryfe with us, and abundance doe dye daylye as I could tell you, but you know them not, I marvayle when I shall make a Iorney into Lanc: to take pleasure, and hunt, and make mery, and not have my gutts Iogd out, and my grease melted with the tediousness of a hott Iorney, and after wearyed with toylesome labour, frō morning untill night, as bad as a day labourer, and when shall I wryte a mery lr̄e, and not alwayes thus of dissentions, Brawles and wranglinge, have I beene bred or used to Iarringe?[80] or take I any delyght in West[mr] Hall, let no man flatter me but tell me playnelye w[ch] way I can doe lesse, except I will suffer both my self, and him that is dead, and the Children to be abusd and wrongd, for the Owldams, I shall take care ere this Terme passe,

---

[78] 'your brother,' i.e., Wm. Seddon at Chester.

[79] 'Robt. Bolton,' a contributor to the chapel fund; 'the one nearer the chapel,' was probably Jas. Oldham, who would not pay his contribution, and whose barn was close to the chapel. (See No. 1.)

[80] 'Jarringe,' i.e., quarreling. So Spenser writes:

> "When those renowned noble peers of Greece,
> Through stubborn pride among themselves did jar,
> Forgetful of the famous golden fleece.
> Then Orpheus with his harp their strife did bar."

and for your mother in law, what hath she to doe to Indent[81] whether y^t 5*l.* be to the Chappell or to ye Scoole, as longe as that is performed, for wch it was given ; I have done for I am wearye of this drosse ; I com̄ende me to your self your wyfe, your sons and Daughters, not forgettinge once more to thanke you for my good cheere, and so I rest

Your assured frend

Bay: Castle   NATHAN WALWORTHE
Sep: 20, 1638

I am to give you notice that although I wryte Bay: Castle thus, w^tin my lr̄e, yet you must not doe so on ye outsyde but at larg, Baynards Castle

wryte as speedelye as you can to your brother for I desyre that to be dispatched, and I thinke he may send to me from Chester, and not send it to you,

---

XLIV.—*Addressed To my lovinge frend Peter Seddon in the Owtwoode of Pilkington.*

Neighbour Peter,

I have rec^d a lr̄e from Mr Horrox,[82] wch I have breiflye Answered, as I must of necessitie doe yours, the Auditt[83] is now with us, and the officers are mett, and many businesses doe fall upon me at this tyme, your lr̄e[84] is longe, and yet not Idle, nor filled with Tautologies, and vayne repetitions, but to the purpose, and hitts upō my mynd, as if you were in my bellye, I will Inclose his lr̄e in yours, that your takinge a fitt tyme to del it, he may reade it in your hearinge, and so it will answere both him

---

[81] '*to indent,*' *i.e.,* to bargain.   So Shakespeare :
" Shall we buy treason and indent with fears."
1 *Henry IV.*, act i, sc. 3.

[82] '*Mr. Horrox.*' See No. 9, and note.

[83] '*the Auditt,*' *i.e.,* of Lord Pembroke's rents due at Michaelmas.

[84] '*your lr̄.*' Cf. "I am with child," &c., in No. 22.

and you, and save me some labour, I deny not, but that I promissed to put the matter to Indifferent men, and I will not goe from it, you have nominated two, Mr Allen, and Mr Sericant[85] I desyre no better, and as you say to me, put on your spectacles and have patience, so, have you but a little patience, and they shall know my mynd ; for I have no desyre to spend money in law, nor, if I were so bent, have I any to spend, and thus much with ye help of Mr Horrax lr̄e, I hope will be sufficient to answere the first part of your lr̄e,

now for the second part, touchinge the will, you sent me, it was made Mar: 16, 1629, the witnesses, you, and Roger Dickson, when my Cosin (though weake and in payne,) yet knew what he did, and delivered his mynd freely Inough, though it might have beene more fullye exprest, if any thinge be defective heerein, it must be supplyed by the honestye, and fidelitye of those that were about him in his sicknes, and hard his words, and knew his mynd and heerein I must appeale unto you, and to Robt. Seddon, and Rog: Dickson or to any that can say any thinge in that case, this last will was made by Io: Birch, Dec: 2, 1630, witnesses, Pe: Seddō, Adā Iepson, and Io: Birch, this will, was about ye tyme of his death, when extremitie of sicknes, and other distractions, together with the solicitations of Adā Iepson, and Io: Birch, in ye behalf of their sister, might make him to doe any thinge, and this I call Io: Birches will, not his and I should more suspect it, but that I fynd you drawne in for a witness ; and this (if there be any

---

[85] 'Mr. Allen and Mr. Sericant.' For Mr. Allen see No. 14 and note. Thomas, son and heir of Peter Sergeant of Newton, and his wife, Margaret, daughter of Henry Ashurst of Ashurst, in the county of Lancaster. He was born in 1582, and was the first of his family who resided at the Stand, Pilkington, as lessee of the earl of Derby. He died there in 1651, and was buried at Prestwich. Peter Sergeant of Pilkington, probably his son, was subsequently a member of the Presbyterian classis, and possibly he, and not Thomas, was the "Mr. Sergeant" here mentioned (see Dugdale and Booker's *Prestwich*).

Thomas Sargant, gentleman, Thomas ffox, gentleman, and Peter Sergant, gentleman, are the three first names on the List of Protestors in Whitfield within Pilkington, in 1641-2.

materiall difference in the 2 wills, may bringe Io: Birch[86] into ye Starr Chamber,[87]

my honest servant Adam, hath made me pay deare for colours Indeed, but I care not, so all be (as you say) well, but I heare by some, all is not well, they say, the wrytings and sentences[88] are much defaced, and look scurvilye, if it be so, it cannot be helped now, it must be helped an other yeare, and lett it alone till then, and lastlye for the Ouldams, and the rest, I will say no more nether will I wish you to say any thinge, but let them alone and seeinge words will not serve, blowes must, and I will say as the Pope did, if Peters keyes will doo no good Paules sword shall,[89] and so by this tyme, I hope you will thinke, I am not behynd with you, for put this to Mr Horrax lr͞e and you cannot say but I have written as much as you, so saith and so affirmeth

Your frend

Bay: Castle   NA WALWORTHE.
Oct: 18 1638.

·

XLV.—*Addressed To my very lovinge frend Peter Seddon in the Owtwood of Pilkington*

Neighbour Peter, I told you if Peters keyes would doe no good, Paules sword must, I am sory I was driven to take this course, especially with your mother in law, and some others, but I must needs doe it lest I should be thought Partiall, let them

---

[86] '*Io: Birch.*' Apparently an attorney.

[87] '*Starr Chamber.*' For once Nathan is justified in his spelling, if this word is correctly derived from 'Starra' (a corruption of the Hebrew, 'Shetar' or covenant), because the covenants made by Richard I. with the Jews were kept in the king's exchequer at Westminster, hence called the Star-Chamber. The statute, 3 Hen. VII., chap. 1, extended the jurisdiction of this court, whose members were the sole judges of the law, the fact and the penalty. Two years later (1640) the Long Parliament abolished it.

[88] '*writings and sentences.*' See end of Introduction. They are still preserved in Ringley church.

[89] '*if Peter's keyes,*' &c. I think Pope Julius the Second made this characteristic remark.

not blame me, I have wayted 3 yeares (if I may speake it with reverence) as Cryst sayd of the barren figgtree, I have putt 4 in a writt,[90] and 4 in a writt to save charges, and have sent ticketts for every one, I comitt the case of servinge them to you, wch you may doe any sonday, but you must take the first sonday, because they may have tyme to prepare for they must Answere the latter ende of this terme and you must choose such a one to doe it as will come up to make Affidavitt, you may have them all, or the most of them at the Chappell, and show them the original writt, and then give every one his tickett, and I have leaft a blank for Doodsons name wch you must supply and put in, for I know not whether his name be Tho: or Adam, or Iames, for I lost the note that you gave me, and I know not whether I have leaft any out that are behynd, if I have let me know and (if this warning will not serve) they shall heare from me the next Terme,

I had thought to have sent a Sub pœna for Tho: Parr but upō better consideration I did not, because of my promisse to referr it, I have not yet tyme to wryte to Mr Allen, or to Mr Sericant, as I purpose to doe, allthough I need not, for you know my meaninge and can give them as good (if not better) Instructions than I ; this shall be sufficient for the present, this day the Qu: mother[91] is entred into London w^t great pompe and Solemnitie,

---

[90] '4 *in a writ.*' Nathan tried to frighten those subscribers to the chapel fund who were still in arrears by threats of legal proceedings. See No. 47.

[91] '*the Queen-mother.*' Mary de Medici, who came much against the wishes of Charles. However, the king assigned her St. James's Palace as a residence, and the poet Waller thus welcomed her :

> " Great Queen of Europe ! where thy offspring wears
> All the chief crowns, where princes are thy heirs,
> As welcome thou to sea-girt Britain's shores
> As erst Latone, who fair Cynthia bore
> To Delos, was."

But in a little more than two years we find the people had conceived a hatred for the Queen's mother ; every day the multitude surrounded her house loading her with insults and menaces. The Court applied to the Commons, who answered that she had better depart, and voted 10,000*l.* for her journey. The Queen retired to Cologne (May 1641), and died there in the year following in very straitened circumstances.

god send us well ridd of hir againe, I ame still full of busines
and must end and rest

Your thankefull frend

Bay: Castle   NATHAN WALWORTHE
No: 1, 1638

XLVI. — *Addressed To my very lovinge frend Peter Seddõ
in the Outwood of Pilkington*

Neighbour Peter, It is true I owed . . . . . . and I have payd it,
I did it of purpose, to have some bodyes fists about your cares
as well as about myne for I ame sure, I shall not escape Scott
free, but who can help it, I am sure I have stayd longe and
longe, and could gett nothinge, but words, (and of some, badd
words,) I have no Intent, nether is it my mynd to put them to
any charges, therefore if they will pay down the moneye,
the law is Answered and you shall nether need to cause
any to make Affidavit, nor I to take out Attachments ; and
besyds, you need not send to Londō, Affidavit may be made
before any Barō of the exchecquer, and if S^r: Humphrey
Damport[92] come home, this Christmas, he is at hand, if he come
not, Baron Weston,[93] is either in Staffordsh: or in Derbysh: wch is

---

[92] '*Sr: Humphrey Damport.*' Sir Humphrey was probably expected at Trafford
near Stretford, where he occasionally resided with his daughter Penelope, who married
Sir Cecil Trafford of Trafford, and introduced her father's christian name into the
Trafford family. (See *Old Stretford*, by Mr. Bailey.)   Sir Humphrey Davenport of
Sutton, in the county of Chester, was the second son of William Davenport of Bramhall,
by Margaret, daughter of Sir Richard Assheton of Middleton. He became chief baron
of the Exchequer in January 1631, was impeached by the commons for assuming the
king's power to levy ship-money in Hampden's case, and retired from public life (see
Foss' *Judges*).

[93] '*Baron Weston.*' Sir Richard Weston, son of Ralph Weston of Rugby, and
related to Richard Weston, earl of Portland, succeeded Sir James Weston (also a
relative) as baron of the Exchequer in April 1634. In 1637 he obtained a patent from
the king, for fourteen years, for sole making Castile and Venice soap (see *State
Papers*, Domestic series). In 1641 he was impeached by the commons, and disabled
from being a judge "as though he were dead." He died in 1651, and was apparently
not related to Richard Weston who became a baron of the Exchequer in 1680, and
died the following year (see Foss).

not farr off, the worst thinge I lyke is Iosua Dicksons answere ;
it savours of mockinge or geering and I could answere it in the
same kynd if I list, or would spend tyme so Idlye, and had leasure,

I will convert myself to you agayne, and tell you how you
shall be revenged on me, I have beene trobled with many
businesses a great whyle, and never had tyme to wryte either to
Mr Allen or Mr Sericant but the last week I writt, (but breeflye)
and referred them in ye particulers to you, and yet had not tyme
to wryte unto you, now if you doe not stirr in the busines, heerein
you may be revenged on me, for I onelye relye upon you, tell
your wyfe Mr Lever and I have many discourses about those
children, and he and I will doe what we can he is as carefull as
any man can be, I have nothinge els at this tyme to say,

what need you a commission to discharge them, what com̄issiō
have you had all this whyle and yet you have received all that
hath beene rec^d: remember to call in those 2, 10^lls that are due
about candlemas, that they fayle not, and so farewell

                              I am yours,
Novr: Ult^o   NATHAN WALWORTHE
  1638

I have found my note agayne, and I fynd Iohn Holme unpayd,
let me know whether his brother by will charged him to pay it,
or what witnes you have, or how we may bring him in or whether
we can take the same course with him, that was taken with the
rest,

————

XLVII.—*Addressed To my lovinge frend Peter Seddon in the
Owtwood of Pilkington.*

Neighbour Peter, I have conferde with M^r Jo: Holme,[94] about
the 5*l.* given by his brother to the Chapell, he saith, he will pay
the 5*l.* so it may be to the good of the Chappell, as his brother

---

[94] '*Jo: Holme.*' Nathan afterwards caused Holme to be arrested, but as the bequest
was 'for pious uses' and without consideration he could hardly maintain it at common
law, as he found out. (See No. 52.) [R. S. S.]

Intended it, I answere, lett him, show the will and I will under-
take nothinge shall be done contrary to the will of the dead, it
seemes he is afrayd least it goe to the scoole, as some others
were, and is desyre his that whosoever receives it of him may put
in securitie, that if it be not layd out accordinge to his mynd, it
may be restored agayne, I have condescended unto him thus farr,
that if it be not layd out, (I will not say accordinge to his mynd)
but accordinge to the will of the dead, it shall be restorde, I
would have you to yeeld unto him in any reasonable thinge, and
make an end of the busines without any wranglinge or Suit of
law and so for this tyme I comitt you to god and rest

Your lovinge frend

Bay: Castle   NATHAN WALWORTHE.
Dec: 5, 1638.

XLVIII.—*Addressed To my very loving frend Peter Seddon
in the Owtwood of Pilkington.*

Neighbour Peter, the trobles Arysinge in Scotland,[95] and the
feare of what might thereupon follow, hindred my determinatiõ,
so that it will be about St Iames tyde before I shall come, send
no money to me, I have too much alreadye except I could use it
better, and for your Accompts, I will not answere them by wrytinge but by word of mouth, and although the Chappell lands be
questioned, yet, that hinders not but you may call for the rent,
and none of the tenants will denye it, you have the feoffment I
have it not nor any wrytings that you need to care for, I can let
you have none of these wrytings yet, I put in my Answere the
last Terme, we shall see what he will doe this Terme, M^r
Hilton[96] wants money, I beleeue so too, and will want, if he

---

[95] '*trobles in Scotland.*' Shortly before this an English army had advanced to
Berwick, intending to attack the covenanters, but the Scots sent commissioners to
York, where the king was, and concluded a pacification just three days before the
date of this letter. These events would make travelling dangerous.

[96] '*Mr. Hilton,*' i.e., William Hulton, the minister at Ringley.

had 100*l.* more per añn but if the parliament hold,[97] the clargye
wil be taken a ladder staffe lower,

Our newes hath beene alwayes uncertaine, today good tomorrow naught,[98] but your home newes his worst, that both hir
brothers Intendinge so well, and makinge such fayre promisses,
and yet doinge nothinge to ye Chappell she should conclude with
nothinge as well as they,

if the B.B: and Mr Allen, contende with you, feight with them,
you will be able to make your parte in good, I am sure you are
20, to one, you must plead prescriptiō and challenge nothinge but
what you have ever had, and I will leave you together by the
eares and rest

                              Your ever lovinge frend
Bay: Castle   NATHAN WALWORTHE.
    June 21, 1639.

XLIX.—*Addressed To my very loving frend Peter Seddon
        in the Owtwood of Pilkington.*

for your Accounts, I will bringe them with me, and reckon
with you there, and for your last letter sent by Tho: Scoales[99]
wyfe, I will give you no answere but this, if Mr Hiltons money
be not yet received and some body must goe for it, let them stay
till I come, and I will goe with them, but let not Mr Hilton want
money in the meane tyme, this is all you are lyke to get of me
at this tyme

                              NA: WALWORTH.
July 1,
    1639.

---

[97] '*if the parliament hold.*'   The 'short' parliament was summoned the following
April, after an interval of eleven years.

[98] '*naught,*' *i.e.,* bad.   Cf. Shakespeare
                "Beloved Regan, thy sister's *naught*"
                              King Lear, act ii, sc. 4.

[99] '*Tho: Scoales.*'   See Nos. 60 and 64.   In 1641-2 Thomas Scoales of Outwood
"took the protestation."

L.—*Addressed To my very lovinge frend Peter Seddon in y*
Owtwood of Pilkington.

Neighbour Peter,

you have made a fayre discourse of your travayles and Iorney,
Tom Coriat[100] could not have done it better, I am afrayd I shall
come short in my relatiō, when we parted you know Mr Wingate,[1]
and his neighbor undertooke to bringe me towards Hull, and by
the way, come (sayd he) I will show you the Sea, and wee will
goe a great way upō the Sands, and so we did, but he brought
me, circum, circa, that I never knew where I was, till I came to
his house, where I was as well wett as ever I was in all my lyfe,
it was happy for you that you gott in before ye rayne the next
morninge when I should be gone, he had turnde my horse to
grasse, and swore I should not goe that weeke, I swore and
starde as fast as he, at last when he saw me so resolute, he puld
on his bootes, and brought me to Hull where we lay that night,
and though it be a Haven towne, and a towne of fishinge, yet I
had as ill lucke as I had before, I could gett no fish for my
Supper,[2] the next morning I was to take Shipp and ye tyde fell
out so ill, I could not goe A board before 12 a Clocke wch though
it was a great crosse to me, yet this Advantage I gott, I viewed
the Towne, went round about the walls, saw the Bulwarks, fortifications, and canons,[3] planted upō ye walles, and (to say the
truth) it pleased me well, it is a fyne towne and streight aboard

---

[100] '*Tom Coriat.*' Nathan refers to a book entitled *Crudities gobbled up in five months
travel.* Thomas Coryat, the author, was the son of George Coryat, fellow of New
College, Oxford, "much commended in his time for his fine fancy in Latin poetry."
In 1608 Thomas Coryat travelled, on foot, some 1900 miles through France, Ger-
many, and Italy, and on his return hung up his shoes in his parish church of Odcombe,
where they remained till 1702. Coryat published his *Crudities* in 1611, and the year
after started on a ten years' ramble, but died at Surat in 1617. Henry, Prince of
Wales, allowed Coryat a pension and kept him about his person, and Fuller described
him as "the courtiers' anvil to try their wits upon." Coryat's travels were republished
in 1776, in 3 vols., 8vo.

[1] '*Mr. Wingate.*' See No. 25, and note.

[2] '*no fish for Supper.*' An old complaint in watering places.

[3] '*canons planted upō ye walles.*' Three months before this (March 29th) the king

I went, hoyst up Sayle, betweene 12 and 1 a Clocke, and as they say it is not above 6 myle over, but ye wind was full[4] and agaynst us, we danct Selingers round[5] and went in and out that we made it 20 myle, and when we should land, the mariners rañ ye Ship a ground so that it was six a Clocke before we landed and then had I 8 myle to goe, to a place caled Brigge,[6] and it was Markett day, and Chamberlayne, tapster and all were drunke I came in late and could get nothinge for my supper but an egg and yet it cost me 8*d.*, and when I went to my Chamber there was one drunke there too, had not I a pleasant Iorney all this whyle, and knew not one foote of the way, for Mr Wingate and I parted at Hull, the next morninge, I had 20 myle to Lincoln where I dynd, and saw the Towne and the Minster, but it is an ill favoured towne,[7] and stands on the syde of a hill, after dinner I had 16 myle to goe, and my direction was to Ancaster,[8] but I was not

had paid a short visit to Hull and carefully inspected the fortifications. When the commons, by vote (January 1642), secured possession of Hull the town contained 16,000 stand of arms, and the king's attempt to take the town was the first operation of the civil war.

⁴ '*ye wynd was full*,' *i.e.*, strong. Cf. Shakespeare,

"I did never know so *full* a voice issue from so empty a heart."
                                                              (*Hen. IV.*, 4, 72.)
           "A *fuller* blast ne'er shook our battlements."
                                                              (*Othello*, ii, 1, 6.)

⁵ '*Selingers round*,' *i.e.*, St. Leger's Round; an old country dance so called. "Mistress Deborah began to jangle Sellinger's Round and desired Alice to dance an old English measure to the tune" (Scott's *Peveril of the Peak*, chap. 12).

⁶ '*Brigge*.' Nathan would land at Barton, where the Ferry was. Brigg, on the river Ancholme, twenty-five miles north of Lincoln. Market on Thursdays then, as now. The inn was perhaps the Angel, which was still there in the reign of Charles II. Nathan may have been in some danger during his voyage, since the year after (1640), as Mr. Bailey has pointed out to me, Andrew Marvel, father of the poet, and master of the Grammar School at Hull, was drowned, with three others, while crossing the Humber from Hull to Barrow.

⁷ '*an ill-favoured towne*.' Speed, writing in 1676, says of Lincoln, "very antient it is and hath been more magnifical, as by her many over-turned ruins doth appear and far more populous as by Domesday book is seen."

⁸ '*Ancaster*,' a village fifteen miles south of Lincoln, and a little south-west of Sleaford, gave a title to the Bertie family, who were dukes of Ancaster and Kesteven from 1715 to 1809, when the title became extinct.

gotten 3 myle out of Lincolne, but I manfully lost my way, and
hitt upō a Towne called Sleeford, where I had good lodginge, and
there I tooke new directions, for I was too farr out of my way to
Hitt upon it agayne, the next day I had 38 myle to Huntingtō,
through dyvers townes, as Burne, Thurleby, Stow, Deepinge,
Stilton, where I came into my way agayne,[9] wᶜʰ is the high road
betweene Yorke and London, heere I could not loose my way, for
besyds yᵉ townes I hitt upō company, but yᵉ 2 dayes before there
was neither Towne, hedg, bush, nor tree, they burne nothinge but
straw and cow turd, from Stilton, I came to Huntington on
Saterday at night, where I rested Sonday, heere I began to
cheere up myself for I was come into a cuntry where I knew, and
was knowne, and had but 2 dayes Iorney home, but when I was
out of my way, and all alone, and in the midst of my crosses I
never ceased to singe, and make my self as mery as I could frō
Huntington on Monday morning to Harding[10] 32 myle, the next
day beinge Aug: 20, Tewsday, I had 24 my: to Londō where I
aryved safe and well by one a Clocke, horse and man and all ;
and never had any mischance, nor lett by loosinge a horse shew
or losse of any thinge therefore I hope I fared the better either
for yours, or some bodyes good prayers els, and tell whether I
am now in your debt or no, and whether Tom: Coriat could
have made a better relation, I have not written thus much to any
of my frends or kinred, therefore if any desyre to know how I
spedd in my solitary Iorney make them Accquaynted with this
letter, and so I commit you to god with thanks and comendations
both to you and your wyfe for my good cheere, not forgettinge yᵉ
lyke to old and yong Ro: Seddon[11] and Thomas too,[12] so I rest
Your lovinge frend
Aug: 30, 1639.   NATHAN WALWORTHE.

    [9] '*I came into my way agayne.*' Nathan probably lost his way on Nocton Heath at
a place where a pillar now stands for guidance. [J. E. B.] From Stilton to Huntingdon he would travel along the Roman road called Ermine Street. Stilton cheese
did not exist in Nathan's time. It was first made by Mrs. Paulet of Wymondham,
near Melton Mowbray, and sold at the Bell Inn in Stilton for 2*s.* 6*d.* a lb. (See
Paterson's *Road Book.*)

I have concluded my lr̄e, but I have not done, I have somewhat more to say wch I would not have everye one to know, therefore you may cut it away before you show my lr̄e, let me know
as soone as you can what answere you have either frō Mr Hopwood[13] or frō Hoome, or whether there be any hope to get any
thinge frō Robinson, if there be not, let it alone be not too Im-
portunate, it may be if he doe nothinge now, he will doe the more
when he Dyes and he cannot live ever, an other thinge is this, as
it was a foolish parte in Hoolme to del. that Interest money to
Mr Hilton, so I hold it a bold and Sawcy parte in him to receive
it, for what had he to doe with it? and I am sory I had not biden
you, when you payd him his money, to stopp it, and call for it,

[10] '*Harding*' in Herts, a little north of St. Alban's, now written Harpenden, but
pronounced Harden.
[11] '*old Rob: Seddon*,' i.e., Robert Seddon of Kersley. (See No. 2.) "Young
Robert" was Peter's youngest son, baptised at Prestwich in October 1629, and
educated at Ringley School under Mr. Cole, and afterwards at Christ's College,
Cambridge. He then lived for some years in Mr. Angier's family at Denton "for the
benefit of his grave example, pious imitation, and useful converse," and preached at
Gorton. In 1659 Robert Seddon, then vicar of Langley, was arrested in Manchester
for having shared in Sir George Booth's rising, and but for the Restoration would have
been tried for his life. He was ejected from Langley in 1662, and again imprisoned
in 1676, under the Oxford Act, for preaching in Richard Baxter's 'new built' chapel
in Acenden Street. After many wanderings he bought a house and land in Bank
Street, Bolton, and presented it to the Presbyterians, who built a chapel there, of
which he was the first minister. Mr. Seddon died soon afterwards (March 1695), of
palsy, at the house of his brother Peter at Prestolee, where he was born, and he was
buried in Ringley church yard in his father's grave. His epitaph begins:
          " For powerful preaching, fervent love, and prayer,
          Few to this worthy comparable were."
Robert Seddon was a noted preacher in his day, and Oliver Heywood, writing to
Ralph Thoresby in 1702, says, "Mr. Baldwin, Mr. Pendlebury, Mr. Newcome, and
Mr. Seddon, all ancient eminent ministers, dead in one year's time, who made a great
breach in Salford Hundred." (See Calamy—Baines's *Lancashire*, vol. iii, and Orme's
Life of Baxter.)
[12] '*Thomas too*.' Younger son of Robert Seddon of Kersley. In 1645 he gave
evidence against Isaac Allen. He married Maria Walworth at Prestwich in 1651,
and was buried there December 1670.
[13] '*Mr. Hopwood*.' Probably Edmund Hopwood of Hopwood, who married
Dorothy, daughter of Edward Assheton, rector of Middleton.

for you must give account of the Interest as well as of the Prin-
cipall, I say nothinge of my busines knowinge your care, you
may burne this before you shew my lre

<hr />

LI.—*Addressed To my lovinge frend Peter Seddon in
the Owtwood of Pilkington*

Neighbour Peter, these lynes are nothinge but to signifye I
have rec^d: yours by Edmond Wallworke, as also this last by
William fox,[14] I can give you no good account of either, thinges
are not rype, but I should be sory if you should be put to so
foule a Iorney for o^{te} I hope to deale well Inough with him without your so great paynes and travayle, you shall heare more
heereafter, for I heare nothing of him, or of his cominge up, you
should doe well to tell me he is come up, that I may harken
after him, he may perhaps come up, and be gone agayne, and I
never heare of it, this is all I have to say for the present, remayn-
inge as alwayes

Your lovinge frend
Oct: 27 1639.   NATHAN WALWORTHE.

<hr />

LII.—*Addressed To my very loving frende Peter Seddon
in the Owtwood of Pilkington.*

Neighbour Peter, I have rec^d your lr̄e, and the note of the
Articles, I doe not lyke ye Articles, it is true, I was moved to
yeeld unto that Article that she should hold the livinge if she
continued widdow, thinkinge it the readiest way to get hir off,
because she would not be kept frō maryage, but I consider she
growes old, and hath many children, and men will not be so
fond on hir, and to enioy such a livinge what will she not doe?

<hr />

[14] '*William fox.*' Probably the nephew of Thomas Foxe (mentioned in No. 6),
and grandson of William Foxe of the Rhodes, who thus mentions him in his Will
(proved June 14, 1599): "to William, son of my son John Foxe, my signet of gold, to
be kept for him by his said father until he comes to years of discretion."

but I may not consent unto that, it is contrary to the will, and
contrarye to my deed of feoffment, and one of the things I complayne of in my bill ye other is lyke unto this, that she should
have 13*l*. 15*s*., for ye education of ye children,[15] I cannot blame
hir to consent to these 2 Articles, this is an other thinge I complayne of, I am content she shall have that wch is fitt and sufficient according to their yeares, one of them is now 10 or 11 yeare
old, and is able or neer able to deserve meate and drinke for hir
worke, and within 5 or 6 yeare will deserve wages, and shall I
then allow 6*l*. 17*s*. 6*d*., for hir education ? why, sure, you had
beene at Gregoryes,[16] or els you would never have sent me such
Articles as these, your former draught of the case, and ye Petition were good, and I followed your direction, and have sent
downe an order out of the court, wch either my Cosin Wilson or
Hugh Parr[17] will show you, and if it be referred to gentlemen in
ye cuntry and I have none to give them Instructions but you, nor
none to take my part but you, and you serve me thus, I shall be
in a fayre case, I was as well servd in followinge your advyce
about Jo: Holme, I arested him, and he stood out, and Denyed
ye debte, I was driven to goe to councell and to see an Attorney
to Declare, and my councell told me, my Action would not hold
at the Common law, it must either be in ye Chancerye, or by
Comissioners in the cuntry, or els he must be Cyted before the
B^p. who by his ecclesiasticall power may compell him, I have
therefore sent you my Cosins testimony to show to the B:^p, and
you must lykewyse gett the copye of the will, and if nether the

---

[15] '*ye children*.' This refers to the affaires of Martha Walworth, the widow of Ellis
Walworth, and her infant children, to whom Nathan was trustee. (See *ante*, No. 35
and note.)

[16] '*at Gregoryes*.' He probably kept an ale-house. (See No. 33.)

[17] '*Hugh Parr*,' of Kersley, married Mary, niece of Nathan Walworth, who left
him, in his Will, "my new Bible covered with greene velvet," a house and garden in
Fennell Street, and a house in Millgate, Manchester. Hugh Parr and Henry Seddon
of Rivington were sent to the Bury 'classis' as elders of Deane. A Hugh Parr of
Salford, no doubt a descendant, was executor of the Will of Richard Tonge of Tonge,
in Prestwich, dated April 1713, and is mentioned as the loving friend and kinsman of
Robert Seddon of Kersley, in his Will proved in May 1720.

B:ᴘ, nor comissioners, help you, let me know and I will take him in hand once more, he did so greeve and mocke me as never poore man was mockt, and you shall heare he will doe the lyke there, but I care not for that, I doe not blame your advyce, for who would have thought, that a thinge given, whereof there was such testimony, and afterward confirmde by will, had not beene recoverable by the common law? They tell me no, any thinge given in pios vsus, for wᶜʰ there is no consideratiō, cannot, I tooke a great deale of paynes, and lost my labour, and was at great charge for he lay at the further end of Grayes Inn lane, and I hunted him up and downe; least you should thinke I was careles, and would doe nothing, yᵉ charg of Sericants, Councellors, and Attorneyes comes to 16s., and I see no reason but I should be Allowed it out of the use money, but I will doe nothinge wᵗout consent, it is longe since I sent you any newes, I will therefore send you some now, (and it is newes Indeed) we shall have a Parliament, I am weary now, I thinke I am not behynd with you, you need not to Grudge me a letter, god send you a mery Christmas, I recᵈ a submissive lrē frō Mʳ Hilton, wᶜʰ I tooke very well, and have Answered it, farewell,

I am still yours, for all

Bay: Castle   you goe to Gregoryes

Dec: 9, 1639.   NATHAN WALWORTHE.

LIII.—*Addressed To my very loving frend Peter Seddon in the Owtwood of Pilkington.*

Neighbour Peter

you will put me (you say) to no more penance but to reade your longe and blotted lrē, marry, you need not, it is even penance Inough, heere is Io: a Noke, and Io: a Style,[18] have a doe,

---

[18] '*Io: a Noke and Io: a Style.*' Cf.

"a mooting-night brings wholesome smiles
When John-a-Nokes and John-a-Stiles
Do grease the lawyer's satin."

from *The Ordinary* by William Cartwright, who died in 1643.

make a doe, I would some wyse man had the perusall of our lrēs,
and I know not what and all to no purpose, but still, obscurum
pro obscurius, and I am never the wyser, it had beene no more
but to have sayd, you have payd for Christmas 1638, you owe for
Christmas 1639, and at Christm: next you will owe 10*l.* for 1640,
but you goe about w^t circumlocutions, and Tautalogies,[19] you
must goe to Scoole agayne, and lett your Children stay at home,
but where am I? or whither am I goinge? I must chaunge my
note, and alter my tune, what's heere? a lrē dated July 13, at w^{ch}
tyme I was in Oxf: at the Act,[20] mery amonge the Doctors, in
the midst of their Disputations, where I was lyke to have my
belly burst and my ribbs broken in the crowde, my shirt stucke to
my backe, and sweate trickled downe my cheekes, and yet I could
have endured it to this day, but now at my retorne I meet with a
lrē that hath stroken a dampe, and ecīipsed all my Contents, fortune nunquā perpetuo est bona, I must be content, and you must
helpe Hugh Parr to advyse with my Attorney seeinge there is no
body but he now, my cosin wilsō[21] beinge dead, I can wryte no
more at this tyme, but must rest

Your Assured frend

Bay castle,   NATHAN WALWORTHE.
    July 24, 1640.

Virte

I should have written more largelye about my busines but the
Death of my cosin hath put me off the hinges and I am not my
owne man, and the case is well knowne in the Cuntry, I desyre
nothinge but that the will of the dead may be performed, and y^e
Children freed from their bondage, and referr my self (lyke a
Malefactor) to God and the Cuntrye Iterñ Vale,

NA: WALWORTHE.

---

[19] '*Tautalogies.*' But see No. 44 where Peter's style is praised as "not idle nor
filled with tautologies and vayne repetitions."

[20] '*the Act,*' *i.e.*, the Act of Commemoration of Benefactors, where Nathan was
probably in attendance on Lord Pembroke, who was then High Steward, and became
Chancellor of the University, soon afterwards, on the attainder of Archbishop Laud.

[21] '*cosin wilson.*' See No. 25.

LIV.—*Addressed To my very lovinge frende Peter Seddon·*
in the Owtwood of Pilkington.

Neighbour Peter, it is true Iepson[22] complaynd to ye court
that the lease was in my hands and gott an order y^t the lease
should be showed, my Answere was, I had not the lease but the
feofees had it, and if they had a desyre to see it, they might goe
either to Wilson or Parr and see it, or take a copye of it, and to
that end I writt to Wilson above 2 Termes agoe, now, see and
Iudg of the honestye of Iepson, and what reason he had to say
I had the lease, but you see further these are nothinge but delayes to shift off the matter, you know also how I have beene
dealt withall from ye begininge, first, we had a motiō to put it to
Arbitrators at Londō, to Madin, Boardman, Hough, &c: but
Iepson would be the Iudge then, when I came into Lanc: Tho:
Parr would put it to frends, but never did it, then I came into
Lanc: agayne and we had a meetinge or two, and you know how
I was served and thus they take advantage at my simplicitye
and ignorance in the law, and I trust to Attorneyes and Solicitors,
and they, to get money, care not how longe a Suit depend, what
would you have me to doe? can I help these things? although
in my weake Iudgment I see no cause why Iepson, should see
the lease or take a copy of it, yet if he demaund it, let him, if he
doe not, then, let my Cosin Parr[23] send me the lease, and I will
bring it into the court, least he take advantage, my meaninge
was not that you should seeke to wamsley my Attorney, but if
he came to you to conferr about ye choyce of Comissioners,[24] you
should assist him, what needs my Cosin Mary[25] to will me to
make an end of this busines, does she thinke I take pleasure in
wranglinge? let her goe to my Attorney and scratch out his
eies, because he makes not an end.

NATHAN WALWORTHE.

Bay: Castle
Sep: 4 1640.

---

[22] '*Iepson*,' mentioned in No. 44.
[23] '*Cosin Parr*.' See No. 52, and note.

LV.

Neighbour Peter, I have rec[d] yours of the latter end of Sep:
by Peter,[26] and for my busines I will doe as well as I can, but
this is not the chiefe cause of my wrytinge, I have an other
thinge in my head wch trobles me, you remember I told you my
resolution about some things for the Scoole and desyred you to
keepe it secrett, and you know what hinderd that it had not
beene done, viz : because it was not leased out for 10*l*. per añ :
the fellow that is in it hath no lease of it, but is in danger to be
turnd out of it everye houre, I am So farr off, and ye fellow takes
advantage thereof, and I have trusted Mr. Wingate[27] in it, and
he does nothinge, and the tymes have beene troblesome, and
Corne Good Cheape,[28] and he is loth to rayse the rent although
I was told it was worth 10*l*., and I gave for y[e] purchase after the
rate of 10*l*., for so everye one tolde me it was really worth, but
now heere the Danger, I may Dye whyle I am expectinge to
make it 10*l*., the questiō is now whether it will not be better for
me to Assigne it over as it is, and leave the improvement to y[e]
feofees[29] heereafter, when the tymes grow better, or els to let it
stand as it doth till I can doe it, and in the meanetyme pay 5*l*.
per añ as I promissed, if you hold it best, I doe it now, before
the night come when no man can worke, Io: 9, 4, then my second

---

[24] '*ye Comissioners*,' *i.e.*, Mr. Allen and Mr. Serjeant.   See end of No. 57, where
Mr. Walmesley is again mentioned.

[25] '*Cosin Mary.*'   See No. 52, and note.

[26] '*Peter.*'   'Neighbour' Peter's eldest son, baptised at Prestwich in April 1617.
He is said to have been present at Lord Derby's execution, but, according to a local
tradition, did not join with some of his family in wishing to plan a rescue.   Perhaps
he considered the sentence justified by the 'Bolton massacre,' on 28 May 1644, when
no fewer than four of his name were killed by the Cavaliers, viz., Henry, Roger,
Arthur and Arthur's wife, Katharine Seddon, a member of the Crompton family,
"zealous and pious Puritans."   (See Register of St. Peters, Bolton, and *Civil War
Tracts*, edited by Dr. Ormerod.)

[27] '*Mr. Wingate.*'   This refers to the Benton estate, which Nathan purchased as
an endowment for the minister at Ringley and the school.   (See his Will and No. 25
and note.)

[28] '*good cheape.*'   Cf. French *bon marché*, and "better cheape," (No. 21).

[29] '*The feofees.*'   The trustees have always been the same for school and chapel.

questiõ is, who ye feofees shall be, whether the same that are to
ye Chappell, and whether it be needfull to have so many, if not
so many, who is fittest to be left out? furthermore because 9, or
10*l*. wil be but a small stypend for a Sufficient Scoo: m^r: how
shall he help him self? of whom shall he receive wages? of any
w^tin the Chappellrye, or of strangers? I would not have any of
the Chappellrye to pay any thinge, especiallye those y^t have
contributed, I cane move 100 questions more, wch I am not able
to Answere, and this is not a sleight thinge and to be dalied
with, it is requisite therefore that you come up and solve this
busines your self, and see it performed as it ought to be, and so
shall I be at quyet, and I hope all you In some parte eased;
and all pleased, I leave it to you to thinke on upõ your Pillow,
and when you have well Deliberated retorne an Answere to

Your lovinge frend

NATHAN WALWORTHE.

if you have well perusde my bill of complaynt I pray you send
it me agayne, this Inclosed lre requyrs your help in the deliverye

Iterũ vale.

Bay: Castle
   Oct: 9, 1640.

LVI. — *Addressed To my verye loving freind Peter Seddon at
his house in the Owtwoode of Pilkington.*

Neighbour Peter,

   I cannot, nor was never wont to Complem^t, and nowe much
less am I being soe weake as I am, you com upon me wth such a
deale of prayses and extollacõn that I know not howe to answer
your lre, but in shorte, to com to the Matter, I have received
your Poake of Meale, wch is as you say 61^li. I never knewe
Oatmeale, sould in Lancashire by weight, but by the heepe or
by the Pocke,[30] why then did not you send me word what it is

---

[30] '*poke*,' *i.e.*, a pouch or bag, a word now replaced by its diminutive pocket.   Cf.
"a pig in a poke" (an expression used by Chaucer), and Shakespeare,

" And then he drew a dial from his poke."

(*As you like it*, act ii, sc. 7.)

by measure, that I may knowe what I must paye for it, But as
you calc to Iohn Horrax [31] for money for the Poake and Carriage soe call to him for money for the meale—soe much for y^t ;
Now must I com to you aboute another busines, here is my
Attorneye [32] com to me wth Comissions and [I know] not what,
hee would have me to give him direction, ... and I knowe
noe more then my katt,[33] I have therefore sent him unto you, to
have dirccõns, I have named, Mr. Allen, and Mr. Sariant for
Comissioners, you knowe what I complayne of, that wheras Parr
gott leave, of me, to tarrye two yeare, promising then to Departe,
and entered in a 100l. bond soe to doe, one of the feofees, Contrarye unto the mynd of both the other, and myne too, gave him
a longer tyme wherby hee hath continued there, ever since, Contrarye to the will of ye dead and contrarye to my will, and contrarye to the custome of the Lordshippe and contrary to all
right and reason, The same feofee Birch by name, hath caused
the other feofees, to seale to a Deede wherin they are bound, to
lett the widdowe have the one halfe of the Living to bring up
the Children ; untill they com to the Adge, of 21 yeares ; wheras
I hope the children are already att that yeares, that they are
able, to gett their living them selves wthout spending of there
meanes, and if the halfe of the livinge should goe to the further
augmentacõn of there porcõns, further, the same feofee hath done
contrarye to my deede ; for I by Deede granted, that my Cosin
Nathan should use halfe of the ground for the good of the Children, and not the widdowe to meddle wth it, you knowe all these
things as well as I : I will wryte noe more aboute it, but leave it
unto you, I hope you are not whyte livered, nor feare the faces,
of a Iepson, Birch or a Iohn Walworth or any woman : I am
still as you left me, verye weake, I was brought to soe lowe, and
to such extreamityes that I have much adoe to recover strength
and soe wth commendacons to your selfe, your wiffe and the

---

[31] '*Iohn Horrax.*' (See next letter and No. 9.)
[32] '*my attorney,*' *i.e.*, Mr. Walmesley.
[33] '*my katt,*' internal evidence that Nathan was an old batchelor.

scoolemayster, wth desire of your prayers I comitt you to god
and rest

Your loving friend

Baynards Castle   NATHAN WALWORTH.
Decem 3^d 1640.

LVII.—*Addressed To my loving freind Peter Seddon in the
Owtwoode of Pilkington.*

Neighbour Peter

  I am not yet able to write a lr̄e to you wth my owne hand,
my weaknes, swelling, and lamenes, Continues wth me still, I
pray you goe to Mr. Richard Lomax[34] and cale to him for nyne
pound and hee will pay it you, You knowe what to doe wth it, it
is Given by will to such a purpose, and I need not to paye it till
I am Dead, but yet notwithstanding I will paye it whylst I am
liveing, and after this tyme, they that goe for the Chappell
moneye shall receive it themselves, if there be any cause to have
a deed or a writeing under my hand for it, let it be drawne and
I will sett my hand to it, remember to cale to my cosin Iohn
Horrox for money for the meale, Bagg and Carriage, and send
me the quanty, what it was, Comend me to Mr. Hulton[35] and
tell him I have received his lr̄e but because I cannot write my
selfe I forbeare to answer it, There is Mr. Wamesley gone downe
wth the Comission, but I knowe not to what end for the other
will not Ioyne in Comission and I know not then what I can
doe, it will be a great deale of Charges cast awaye in vayne, but
I leave it to your discretion, when you see Mr. Wamesley, desire
him to send me downe my writings, that I may goe to other
Councell, hee never . . . . . till within two or three dayes of the
Terme, and keepes my writeings and I can make no use of them,
if I had them heere I could advise wth others, and goe one in
somethings without him, therefore let him not fayle to send

34 'Mr. Rich. Lomax.' (See No. 25 and note.)
35 'Mr. Hulton.' The minister at Ringley, whose name is here spelled rightly.

them, Com̄end me to my two Com̄issioners Mr. Allen and Mr. Sariants, Mr. Cole,[36] your selfe and your wiffe and soe I rest

Your loving frend

Baynards Castle NATHAN WALWORTHE.

Decem: 10ᵗʰ 1640.

LVIII. — *Addressed For his Lov: Brother Capt. John Seddon*[37] *at his Quartʳˢ in Cumberland or where ever.*

Kind Brother,

Havinge such an opportunitie, I should not express endeared affection If I should be silent, But as heretofore I have often taken upon me a brotherly bouldnes to use freedom of speech and to wryte my full hart as plainely as if I spoke it in your eare : which, for any thinge I ever knew, you have as Ingeniously accepted of as it was entended, yett once more I must acquaint you wᵗʰ my father's and my owne sence of your present condicōn which in these criticall tymes nothinge but conscience of our dutie of Love and faithfullnes to you could have prevailed with us thus farr to have expressed ourselves. Truly Brother It is no smale trouble, greefe and matter of mourninge to me, and to your parents and Christian freinds, to heare that after the Lord

---

[36] '*Mr. Cole.*' Then schoolmaster at Ringley.

[37] '*Capt. John Seddon,*' the third son of 'neighbour' Peter. I know nothing more of him, but a John Seddon was killed at Bolton about a month later (16 Feb. 1642-3) while fighting under Colonei Ashton to repel the attack of Lord Derby's forces from Wigan. (See Burial Register of St. Peter's, Bolton.) This letter, written by Captain Peter Seddon, with a postscript by 'neighbour' Peter, shows strong family affection, as well as the Puritan leanings of both father and son. Marsden (*History of the Early Puritans*, p. 442) says, "There were few Puritans in the royal army when the war began. The church Puritans were men of peace. Whatever their opinions were as to the lawfulness of an armed resistance, they were extremely reluctant, in this instance, to draw the sword, as they could not identify themselves with either party." 'Neighbour' Peter and his son, though anxious to persuade John to resign his commission in the royal army, avoid direct mention of politics, and rest their argument on the ground that his character as a Christian was injured by the ill-repute of his lieutenant and other officers, who had lately replaced "those faithful to God," that is, men of Puritan opinions whose loyalty to the king was suspected.

hath done so great things for you even to admiration as in som
of your letters your selfe have confessed That you should doe
that wch tendeth so much to gods dishonour and endangereth so
much your owne overthrow, Both w^{ch}, he that hath eyes may
plainely see unavoidably cominge on If by tymely repentance
and reform no prevention bee The matter is your neglectinge
or castinge of those who (you can not but be persuaded) have
beene and are deare and faithfull to god, to the publicke and to
yourselfe, who whylst they were wth you, prayd w^t you and for
you : and I hope were your deare Christian Companions : propps
and pillars : and who knowes how much good god hath done to
you for theire sakes, sure I am you had more prayers for you,
and were more precious in the eyes of gods people then, But
since you parted w^t them how many such have you in your
Companye nay whom have you taken in as next to you : Ah
brother If you knew how much displeasinge this doinge is to
all Christians that love you ; and how much they are greeved
for you ; and what it presageth of you ; it would trouble you
somethinge, as it doth me. If you call to mynd what my father
writt and what I writt, before the thinge was done : and what we
said to you when you were at home, our trouble is encreased :
even morrall men Doe speake evell of you for it but the fears of
Christians are, eyther y^t the worke of grace was never truly and
really begun in you, or els that you are in a declyncinge condic͠on
What Christian in a good frame would have suffred a religious
leiueten^t and a relig͠ ensigne to have gone of who have beene so
faithfull and loveing (especialy when you have none y^t is relig͠
left, I heare of none or y^t will come to you) and all through a
fond conceipt of a very deboyst [38] wicked man : Brother, as they
were a blessinge and a Credit to you : hee is the quyte contrary,
who dare trust such a one. we heare such bad reports of his

---

[38] '*deboyst*,' *i.e.*, debauched.
  "Here do you keep a hundred knights and squires,
  Men so disordered, so debauched and bold."
                                        (*King Lear*, act i, sc. 4.)

Carriage, wickednes Cosenage oppresinge the Contry, enrichinge himselfe by wronge, and that he is to hard for any in the Brigade but one (viz) the black Diṽ : whose right eye he is. my father tould you wherfore (as he thought) such a man was put upon you. I heare the Ma: generall [39] himselfe Disclaimes havinge any hand in it. and w^{t}in these 3 dayes (if the lord will) I will know it of himselfe more perfectly. Your name suffers in all the ill your L^t doth, and how farr you will be found guiltie therof, both before god and men I leave to yours : to Iudge. If you deserve a Companye you deserve to choose your owne officers : but if in all this you be a sufferer, and y^t he bee thrust upon you, and the man himselfe be as the sonnes of Zeruyah to David (too hard for you) wch is all our hopes and plea for you to others, and wch we would faine have more assurance. Then, in gods name acquitt your selfe lyke a man lyke a Christian. Cleare yourselfe to god and to his people to your deare freinds who are mourninge and prayinge for you and expectinge what impression all this will take upon your soule—by castinge of such a Magus, or Elimas ; who when all the good men in your Company are gone, and the rest, bad enough to doe any thinge will turne you of, and have the Company at his owne com̄and if tymes be for it.

Brother If you cannot acquitt yours. herein, no other way you may retyre yours. to your father and friends : and be received w^t Ioy and honour, for all reproch will bee herby wyped away ; and you will be freed. or more freed from the danger you are in : for who knowes what to advyse, or resolve upon And if there be any good occasion for you againe to take up Armes you will have all your old officers and souldiers now at home readie at your service But if no occasion be for them (as for my owne parte I am encorraged to hope) you may (wth the lords blessing)

---

[39] '*the Ma: general.*' Perhaps Sir Thomas Tildesley is here meant. He commanded Lord Derby's troops in the first attack on Bolton, and the writer of *Lancashire's Valley of Achor*, in describing the attack, speaks of Sir Thomas as "the Earle's Major generall." (See Ormerod's *Civil War Tracts.*) In February 1643, major general Sir John Seaton was in command of the Parliament troops at Manchester.

setle yours: you have som guese where, and I could tell you
somethinge wch might be an encorragm^t wch I knew not when I
saw you last. But howsoever you might be at libertie and have
tyme to consider what you did, before you should bee put upon
any engagem^t: wch how desperate a thinge it were (I meane to
engage w^t any syde in these tymes) I can not say. And now
haveinge eased my selfe a litle I pray god to helpe you to judge
arright of your owne way, and what I have writt. And I pray
god it may not dryve you to unprofitable meloncolly, but may
be a meanes to bringe you neerer to him and make you more
humble for your faileing in this particular And the good lord
who hath promised to teach the humble, And to leade the Blynd
in the wayes wherin they should walke, Teach, guyde and Leade
you in his way, to doe and persist in nothinge to his dishonour,
your owne scandall and sin ; and your freinds greefe, But may
doe much for him, and receive much grace from him, wch is and
shall be the prayer of

Your very affec̄ Brother

E patr̄ Dom̄   PETER SEDDON.
Jan: 15th 1642.

Dear John, I Charge you as you expect the prayers or blessing
of your mother and me be advyssed by us your Dearest freinds
and welwishers peruse dilligently what is above written and the
Lord Direct you to walke in the Right way so practh

Your ould father
PETER SEDDON.

Your mother with teares Saluteth you.

Brother, I do heare the Ma: Generall is come to you, I am
disapointed y^t way. I hope he is come to fech you of eich man
to his home. Sooner and better   vale —

LIX.[40]—*Addressed ffor the Reverend Mr John Walker at his
Rectory at St. Maries in Exeter.*

Reverd Sir, In pursuance of a promise I formerly made in a
letter to Mr Webber, I have here sent you ye following account

---

[40] [Contributed by Mr. Bailey.] This interesting letter is without date, but it would
be written about 1710. The gentleman to whom it was addressed was the laborious
compiler of that very valuable work, notwithstanding its many faults, entitled *An
Attempt towards recovering an Account of the Numbers and Sufferings of the Clergy of
the Church of England, &c., in the late Times of the Grand Rebellion.* London, 1714,
fo. It was to aid in the preparation of that work that Mr. Seddon's letter (in reply to
a circular letter of Dr. Walker's) was written; and its substance will be found em-
bodied in the account of William Seddon, given in pt. ii, pp. 351-3, of the *Attempt.*
Walker's *MS.* correspondence was given to the Bodleian Library, in accordance with
his publicly expressed resolve to preserve his vouchers in testimony of his integrity,
and to place them in some public repository "whenever it shall please god to call me
off" (p. xlvii). His papers did not come to the Bodleian until 1754 or 1756; and
they have of late been arranged in twenty-three vols., in folio and quarto, arranged in
counties (Maoray's *Annals of the Bodl.,* p. 167). It is to be gathered from the correspondence, that so early as 1705 Walker was busy in the prosecution of enquiries in
all parts of the country. His account of the preparation of his great work is a piece
of literary history of surpassing interest. "The bare Register of *Memorandums* of
of what Things I was to Enquire after, whom I was to write, or Apply myself to, who
had Answered me, &c. Amounted to a Volume." He adds, that the letters he wrote,
the collections, transcripts, &c., that he made, and the copy for the press, amounted
to near twenty reams of paper (pp. xlix and 3). John Walker, of whom no full and
accurate account is to be found in the existing biographical dictionaries, was the son
of Endymion Walker, mayor of Exeter in 1682, and was baptized in S. Kerrian's
parish in that city 21 January 1673-4. He was sent to Exeter college, Oxford, and
matriculated there, 19 November 1691. Four years later he was elected a fellow of
his college. On 22 August 1698 he was admitted rector of S. Mary Major's church
(called "Mary's the More" on the title-page of *The Attempt*), Exeter, void by the
death of the Rev. Richard Carpenter. He became M.A. 13 October 1699. When
Calamy published his *Account* of the ministers ejected for nonconformity, Mr. Walker
undertook a similar work for the Church of England, and it was published in 1714.
The University of Oxford presented him with the diploma of D.D., 7 December 1714,
"as the most proper and reasonable mark of respect without doing exercise or paying
fees." On 17 October 1720 this learned divine was admitted rector of Upton Pyne,
vacated by the death of James Gay, clerk, on the presentation of Hugh Stafford of Pyne,
Esq., the father of the paternal great-grandmother of the present Right Hon. Sir
Stafford Henry Northcote, Bart. At Upton Pyne, it appears, the Rev. Doctor died.
He was buried on the north side of the church-yard, 20 June 1747, aged 73. His
widow, Martha (Brocking), was buried on the 12th of the following September,
aged 67 (Dr. Oliver's *Ecclesiastical Antiquities,* vol. ii, p. 54; Cooper's *New Biog. Dict.*)

of my most honoured Father's sufferings in the late times of rebellion and confusion, wherein, though perhaps, I may be under some mistakes, in not adjusting every passage to it's proper time, or mis-nomen of some persons mentioned in it, yet I have not wittingly and knowingly trespas'd upon y⁰ truth in any material part of my relation, which I hope you'l therefore peruse with candour as follows :

The Reverend Mʳ Willm. Seddon (my most honoured Father) M.A. of Magdalen Coll, in Camb, being about the year of our Lord 1636, setl'd a preacher in one of y⁰ parish churches, I think St. Maries, in y⁰ City of Chester, was then also possess'd of a Vicarage at Eastham (about six miles distant from y⁰ City, value 68ˡⁱ per annum) where he lived with his wife and family in a very happy condition, till y⁰ Civil war's breaking out, and y⁰ Parliament forces drawing on to besiege Chester, he was compel'd to withdraw his family and effects into y⁰ City for succour, where his great and good friend and Pastor y⁰ Lord Bishop Bridgeman, then Lord Bishop of Chester, accommodated him with several rooms and lodgings in his own Palace ; and yet the aged Bishop dreading the hardships of a siege, voided the place, leaving my Father in his Palace, who continued diligent in his ministry, and frequent Preaching to y⁰ Garrison there. And the City being closely besieg'd and frequently stormed, my Mother was on y⁰ 12ᵗʰ day of Octob. 1645 delivered of me her 9ᵗʰ child, (all the 9 then living) and said to be y⁰ last yᵗ was publickly baptiz'd in y⁰ Font of yᵗ Cathedral there before y⁰ restoracion in 1660. The City being surrendred upon Articles my Father was shortly apprehended and made Prisoner, and after some short durance was demanded by y⁰ prevailing Powers, why he had not, according to y⁰ Articles of surrender, march'd off with y⁰ Garrison to y⁰ King's Quarters, to which he reply'd, yᵗ he thought his cassock had unconcern'd him in those Articles, being a Minister in y⁰ City, but above all he had a wife, and many small children there, which if he could see tolerably dispos'd of he would, not unwillingly, accept the Articles. But many complaints being made against him, y^t he had in his preaching reflected upon the proceedings of the prevailing party, and had animated ye Garrison to resist even unto blood &c, he was remanded to Prison again, and his house permitted to be plunder'd by ye souldiers, who despoild him not of his goods only, but of his books and papers, which they exposed to sale at a very low rate ; and so by private directions to some of his friends, he repurchas'd some of the most necessary for his own use.

But then an order was drawn up to export his wife and children out of ye City to Eastham (which accordingly was done, several of ye younger sort being put into a wagon with other goods which had escap'd the pillage) where though they had only ye bare walls of a Vicarage house to resort to, yet they found a hearty welcome from ye loial part of the parishioners there, amongst whom they dispers'd themselves, and in a short time after, my Father's confinement was somewhat enlarg'd, and his escape conniv'd at, which gave him ye liberty of going in quest of his wife and children, whom he found in pretty good circumstances amongst his loial friends.   But another minister (whose name and character I have utterly forgot) being dispatch'd with orders from ye ruling powers at Chester to supply the vicarage at Eastham, and a rumour dispsd, y^t my father must be apprehended again and reduc'd as prisoner to Chester, he scamper'd about privately to the houses of ye loyal Gentry, to whom his character and condition were well known, and then despatched a letter to his elder Brother Mr Peter Seddon at Outwood in Lancashire (ye place of my Father's nativity) who was then, at that rate of ye times, turn'd zealous Presbiterian too, and had a son a Captain in ye Parliaments army, acquainting him with ye storm he was under, and requesting him to cover either all or part of his ffamily, till he could weather ye storm ; to which letter ye main of ye answer he had was y^t would he conform himself to ye Godly party, his own merits would protect and prefer him, which so insensed my Father y^t he never more held any correspondence with him.

But in his perambulacons amongst yᵉ loialists, conducted by
yᵉ good hand of Providence, he met with one Mʳ Bratherton,[41] a
Lancashire gentleman and a hearty Cavalier, with whom he had
former acquaintance, and who by virtue of a deed of trust from
one Mʳ Byrom, a gentleman, yᵗ was slain in the King's service,
had the donacon of a Parsonage call'd Grapenall (which was
then vacant by yᵉ death of one Mʳ Richardson its incumbent)
and the presentacion to this Rectory he freely tendered to my
Father perswading him, with all possible secrecy and expedicon,
to post up to yᵉ Commissioners or Tryers of Ministers, which
accordingly my Father did, and upon examinacon was by them
approv'd and recommended to yᵉ Rectory of Grapnal, a Parsonage worth about 130ˡⁱ per annum, at 16 or 18 miles distance
from Chester and bordering upon Lancashire.

Here he settled and fix'd himself, well accepted and beloved
by his Parishioners so yᵗ he had time to recollect his dispersed
Family and enjoy'd a calm ; but this could not be durable, he
was soon haunted with the old rumours of a dangerous delinquent
a malignant &c, and this grew up into menaces of articles and
complaints and at last into a moral assurance yᵗ one Major Brooks
a Parliamenteer officer (whose malice he had formerly experi-
enced) intended to seize and apprehend him, which caused him
for a time to abscond and afterwards, upon overt attempts made
upon him, to flee into Lancashire, where he was by some friends
recommended to one Mʳ Fleetwood[42] of Penwortham (a parish
situate near to a great market town called Preston, and about 22

---

[41] '*Mr. Bratherton.*' John Bretherton of Hey, who, by his marriage with Isabel,
widow of John Byrom of Byrom, became the step-father of Henry Byrom here mentioned. Henry Byrom fell at Edgehill, 23 October 1642, while fighting on the king's
side under Lord Molineux.

[42] '*Mr Fleetwood.*' From the *Parliamentary Inquisitions* in the Lambeth Library
we learn that Penwortham was styled a parish in 1650, and the tithes, paid in kind,
were valued at 174*l.*, which "Mr. John Fleetwood of Penwortham, Esq.," claimed as
his inheritance. Mr. William Seddon was then the "preaching minister," having
been "put in" by Mr. Fleetwood with the consent of the parish, and his stipend-wages
was 60*l.* a year. Mr. Fleetwood married Anne, daughter of William Farrington of
Werden, and died in 1657.

miles distant from Grap'nall in Cheshire) who being a very loial gentleman and impropriator of ye tyths of y^t parish, entertained him in ye quality of a chaplain, or curate, to preach at y^t little church near adjoining to Penwortham Hall.

Here my father fixed again in this gentleman's house, entirely beloved of his patron (who allowed him 40^li per annum) and of all his parishioners and having intelligence out of Cheshire, y^t my mother, whom he had left at Grap'nall with a strict charge to gett ye place supply'ed and keep possession as long as she could, was with her family ejected ye Parsonage house there and a new Rector one Mr Bradshaw, a rigid Presbyterian (whether by appointment of commoners or usurpacon I know not) put in, he acquainted his Patron Mr. Fleetwood with it, who thereupon order'd a poor cottage house at a little distance from his own Hall, to be fitted up and added 3 or 4 acres of ground to't, to keep a couple of cows and here, as in a little ark of rest, my Father seated himself with his wife and 9 children, supported and maintain'd by ye good hand of Providence, which order'd him still ye 40^li pension from his Patron and large gratuities from ye Loyalists in those parts, whose children he privately baptiz'd and performed other ministerial offices, at their requests, according to the antient forms of ye church; which tho' it gave him sometimes ye trouble of musquetiers to guard him into Preston as a Prisoner, yet upon ye mediacon of the neigh'bring Gentlemen he was soon dismissed and return'd to his family to recount his hazard, with his olim meminisse juvabit; and tho' in all this time he had not any allowance of a 5th, or any ye leest part from either his Parsonage or vicaridg in Cheshire, nor any temporal estates whatever, yet he liv'd cheerfully and contentedly and saw many of his children comfortably dispos'd of and presently upon ye Restoracon in 1660, he ejected Bradshaw again, who though a rigid Presbyterian yet he then trim'd up and got another benefice call'd Lym in Cheshire, where I think he dy'd.

And my Father being restored to his Rectory at Grapnall resetl'd himself and his family in the parsonage house there, where he and my mother (y^t constant partner of his sufferings) aged each of them about 70 years, departed this life, both in one month and lye buried both in one grave in the chancel there A.D. 1671.

Thus S^r I have recounted those sufferings wherein you'l find me not altogether unconcern'd and tho' by reason of my minority and ye lack of memoirs in writing (for I was in ye station I now am at ye death of my Parents and so could not have my fathers notes) I have made but an imperfect relation of them yet I dare avouch ye truth of my relation as to all ye material and substantial parts of it, for I was born nurs'd and train'd up under those dispensacons, which I think may be allow'd good and even sensible, grounds in me for belief of what I have writt and render it unsuspected by men of candour and ingenuity ; and now if upon your perusal of this paper you find anything, which you adjudg incoherent or impertinent, pray cancel and cover it; but if anything worth publick notice, pray make use of it, and may God succeed your endeauours to his own glory, and that peace and unity of the divided church is the hearty praier of,

S^r

yor. assured Friend and affectionate Br. in the Lord

EDWARD SEDDON.

If you think fitt to move any further queries about ye p'misses transmit them by Mr Webber.[43]

---

[43] '*Mr. Webber.*' "Nicholas Webber of Exon., gent.," appears upon the list of subscribers to Walker's *Sufferings of the Clergy.* He was the Registrar to the Archdeacon of Exeter (cf. Calamy's *The Church and the Dissenters Compar'd, as to Persecution,* 8vo, 1719, p. 8).

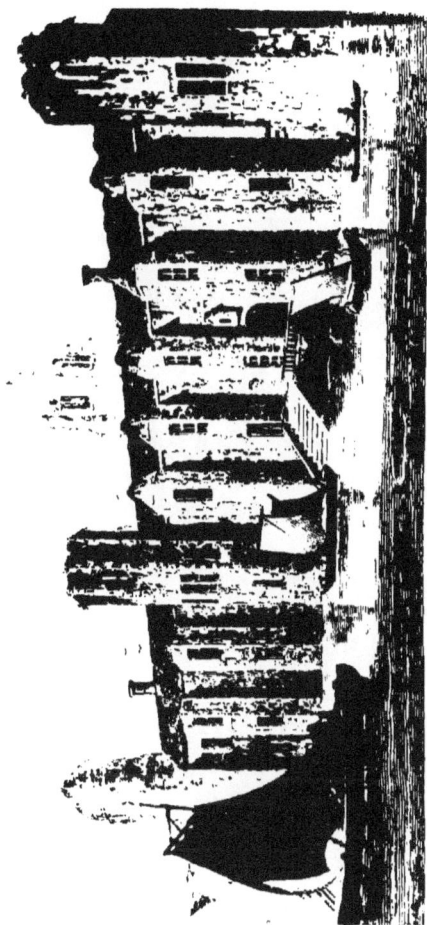

BALVENIE CASTLE, BANFF

APPENDIX.

LX. — *The names of the Contributors,*[44] *who gave their* 5*l. and have a right to Pews in Ringley Chapel.*

Ellis Walworth	£5	Michael Seddon	£5
Geo. Murrey	5	Ellis Farnworth	5
John Horrocks	5	John Ouldham	5
John Grundie	5	William Seddon	5
Peter Seddon	5	John Walworth	5
Robt. Boulton	5	Josua Dickson	5
Ellis Walworth	5	Robt. Seddon	5
James Oldan	5	Rich. Heap	5
Hugh Parr	5	Thomas Scoales	5
Rich. Fletcher	5	John Barse	5
Widdow Doodson	5		

Apud Lever 19 August Anno 1634.

In performance of the above said Promise the parties above mentioned (so many as are now living and the rest of them by their Executors) except James Oldham came to the Lord Bpp of Chester the day year and place last above written and gave and delivered into his hand the said several sums respectively (except the said James Ouldham) five pounds as they are above written to the use aforesaid whereof the said Bpp being possessed and themselves utterly destitute of anie right or property therein he did then and their pay over the whole sum amounting to 100*l.*

[44] Most of them have been mentioned in previous notes. Geo. Murray, the rector of Bury, died the year before (1633). Ellis Walworth was the younger son of Nathan's brother Peter; he died in 1630, and left the 5*l.* as a bequest, as did also William Seddon, Peter's father-in-law. The second Ellis Walworth, probably a cousin, was churchwarden of Prestwich in 1641. Richard Fletcher perhaps belonged to a family of that name at Stoneclough, mentioned in the Will of William Hulme, proved in 1637. In 1641-2, Richard Fletcher of Outwood took the Protestation.

into the hands of Peter Seddon Robt Seddon Thos. Parr John Walworth John Horrocks of Pilkington and Josuah Dickson of Clifton to be forthcoming from time to time upon three months warning given to them or anie of them their heirs Exōrs or Administrators by the said Lord Bpp or anie of his successors Bpp of Chester for a stock to be imployed for the wages of the Ministers there successively or toward the purchasing of some certainty annualy for the same and for no other use

Witnesses here unto

LAW. BOOTH
THO. WASH   JO: CESTRIEN
WILLM TEMPEST

LXI.—*Abstract of Sentence of Consecration of Ringley Chapel signed by Bishop Bridgeman, June 1st, 1635.*

To all our faithful and well beloved in Christ to whom these presents shall come Iohn Bishop of Chester sends greeting

Be it known to you that on Thursday September the 11th 1634 betwixt the hours of one and three in the afternoon at the door in the entrance of the Cemitary of the Chapel below specified personally appeared before us Thomas Fox and Nathan Wallworth the younger of Pilkington gentleman who by virtue of a Letter of Attorney from Iames Lord Strange eldest son and heir of William Earl of Derby lord of the Manor of Pilkington and from Nathan Wallworth of the city of London Gentleman at whose sole cost the said Chapel was built Resigned into our Hands for pious uses the same Chapel and Cemitary which Resignation by them publicly read and then given into our hands is as follows

We Thomas Fox and Nathan Wallworth of Pilkington yeomen being authorized ·by the said Lord Strange and Nathan Wallworth of London do offer into the hands of Iohn Bishop of Chester the said House and Ground and We beseech his Lordship to consecrate it to the service of God   In Witness whereof we have set our Hands and Seals December 11th 1634

Wherefore We the said Bishop determined to proceed to the Consecration of the same having first pronounced a Blessing upon the Founder and a curse upon all such as shall in future times presume to injure the same   And having entered the Chapel shut out the people and locked the door took possession of the same in the Name of the Father of the Son and of the Holy Ghost and pronounced that the Right and title of the said Lord Strange and Nathan Wallworth and of their Heirs to the said Chapel and Cemitary hereafter be null and void

Immediately after this the door being opened and the people let in we sitting in a certain place for us prepared Read public prayers according to the custom of the Church of England with Psalms 84 122 and 123 and 5th chapter of the 2nd Cor and 21st chap of Matt from verse 12 with the Litany Decalogue and part of the 10th of Hebrews from verse 19 to verse 29 for the Epistle and the 19th of Revelations to verse 9 for the Gospel, which done being seated in a chair in the sight of the people there sitting We dedicated and consecrated the said chapel and appointed it for the celebrating of divine service and preaching the Word of God and Read in manner following Whereas Master Nathaniel Wallworth hath at his own proper costs erected this Chapel containing within walls 13 yards in length and nine in breadth together with the chancel annexed containing 5 yards in length and 6 in breadth together with the adjacent cemitary and hath furnished the same Chapel with a pulpit and Communion Table for the receiving the Lord's Supper a Bell[45] convenient seats and other things necessary for divine worship And Whereas the inhabitants of Ringley Kersley Clifton and Outwood have given a perpetual yearly Stipend for a Minister invested with Priest's orders to officiate there continually

[45] 'a Bell.' This bell has the initials S. R. E. K. inscribed on it. I can offer no explanation of them. The Rev. T. N. M. Owen, vicar of Rhodes, obtained the rubbing, at some risk to himself.

And Whereas the Inhabitants have besought us to consecrate
the said Chapel to divine uses We therefore Iohn by divine
providence Bishop of Chester Decree and Declare the place to
have been so consecrated and that it ought to be called by the
name of Saint Saviour's Chapel and so we name it and it is our
Will that the same Chapel be secured in all its Rights and
Priviledges Compatable to the Chapel of this kind (saving
always the Right and Interest of the Mother Church of Prestwich Eccles and Dean their Tythes Rights and Priviledges whatsoever) and we grant by these presents leave to the Inhabitants
of Ringley Kersley and Outwood to come to the said Chapel and
there to offer up publick prayers to God and to hear Sermons
We give also to Nathan Wallworth aforesaid during the term of
his natural life power of nominating and presenting to us and
our Successors Bishops of Chester some learned honest and
fit Presbiter to serve the Cure of the said Chapel but after his
Decease we grant the same Right of Patronage to the Rector of
Prestwich Bury and Middleton for the time being or to the major
part of them forever Reserving also always to ourselves and
Successors not only the power of admitting and approving the
said Presbyter but also if need be and just cause appear of re-
moving him reserving also to ourselves and Successors the sum
of one shilling for the annual meeting of the Clergy to be paid at
the ffeast of Easter according to the Right and Custom of this
Diocese and in like manner the sum of two shillings to be paid
at every Triennial Visitation to us and our Successors for pro-
curation Which things being thus finished We offered up our
prayers to God for the acceptance of the aforesaid work and
dismissed the Congregation with a blessing

In Testimony whereof we caused our Episcopal Seal to be
affixed to these presents June 1st 1635 in the 17th year of our
Consecration.

                                        IO: CESTRIEN.

LXII. — *Abstract of the Indenture of Endowment of Ringley Chapel, dated 23 June 1635. Between Nathan Wallworth of London on y̅e̅ one part and Nathan Wallworth and John Wallworth of Ringley Peter Seddon Richard Heape John Horrock and Robt. Seddon of Pilkington co. Lanc. yeomen hereinafter called the Trustees on the other part.*

The Indenture recites the building and consecration of Ringley chapel, and thus proceeds :

Now Witnesseth these presents that y̅e̅ said Nathan Wallworth being very desirous that y̅e̅ cure should be officiated by a godlic learned preacher of y̅e̅ Word of God who shall not only read divine service therein twice every Sunday but also preach unto such as shall resort to y̅e̅ said Chapel and that all the rents of the lands hereinafter mentioned shall be employed for the maintenance of the said preacher doth hereby grant to the said trustees and their heirs all those 84 acres in Little Benton co. York now in the occupation of Isabell Robinson and all those 40 acres in Little Benton aforesaid now in the occupation of John Norham and all Fowling and taking of Fowle upon y̅e̅ cliffes in Little Benton near y̅e̅ sea to such uses as is before herein mentioned.

The Indenture concludes with a provision for the appointment of fresh trustees.

NATHAN WALWORTH.

Signed sealed and delivered
   in y̅e̅ presence of

(L. S.)

J. WHITE
GEO. BILLINGHURST.
JNO. WADE

Recognovit coram me
   JOHANNE MYCHILL
   23rd June 1635.

LXIII. — *Abstract of the Will of Nathan Walworth.*

In the name of God Amen the fifteenth day of October A.D. 1640 I Nathan Walworth of London gent being weak in body but of perfect mind and memory laud and praise be given to Almightie God therefore and calling to mind the uncertainty of this transitory life and knowing that death is certain and the hour thereof most uncertain do therefore make this my last will and Testament First and principally I commend my Soul and Spirit into the hands of Almighty God my heavenly father most assuredly trusting through the meritts of the most pretious death and bloudy passion of his most dearly beloved sonn our only Lord and Saviour Christ Iesus to obtain free pardon and forgiveness of all my sins and offences and to enjoy eternal rest amongst the chosen and elect people of God in his most blessed and glorious kingdom And my wretched body I committ unto the earth from whence it came in an assured hope of a most joyfull resurrection the buriall whereof I will to be such as becometh a Christian according to the good direction of mine Executors hereafter named

And as touching the disposition of all such worldly estate as it hath pleased God of his infinite goodness to bless me withall I devise and bequeath the same as followeth

Unto Sara Walker the daughter of my sister Sara deceased the Somme of twentie pounds Unto my cozin Hugh Parre my new Bible covered with greene velvet and all my estate and interest in all that house parlours or chambers situate in Fennell Street Manchester and all that house shop and stable in Milgate Manchester which premises in Fennell street and Milgate I hold of James Lord Strange during the lives of Thomas Heape son of Thomas Heape of Pilkington James Wilsonne son of William Wilsonne of Prestwich and John Parre son of Hugh Parre of Kersley And I bequeath to my niece Mary wife of the said Hugh Parre tenne pounds To my cozen Hester Wilson tenne pounds and to her sonnes all my Latin books All my estate for three lives called Babiles at Brockerbanke co. Lanc. to my cozen Nathan Walworth and his assigns And I also give him all my English books To my cozen Peter Walker five pounds And to his wife five pounds To my cozen Anne Chetham [46]

[46] '*Anne Chetham.*' Probably a relative of Humphrey Chetham, as Canon Raines informed me that Humphrey contributed £c⁵ towards the Chapel fund.

five pounds To my cozen Elizabeth Higgenson five pounds To my cozen George Brooke fortie shillings To my cozen John Openshawe[47] the sonne of James Openshawe fortie shillings To my cozen Samuel Walworth[48] now of Oxford tenne pounds To my loving freind Sir Matthew Lyster[49] knight tenne pounds and two pictures one of Philoclea and Pamela and the other of the Spawe[50] To Thomas Waterworth and his wife a silver spoone guilt And to their eldest son Nathan my godson fortie shillings To Mistress Darnelly my silver Sloap: pott weighing twentie ounces To Mistress Williams of Ampthill a silver tonne weighing six ounces To my aforesaid cozen Hester Wilson all my interest in a tenement newly builded in Ramm's Alley in the parish of St. Dunstan in the West near the Inner Temple London To Mr. Anthonie Hinton an Indian nutt trimmed with silver like a bottle with a cover To the right wor[ll] my very

[47] '*John Openshawe*' of Radcliffe, who married Margaret, daughter of Robert Radcliffe of Radcliffe. (Dugdale.)

[48] '*Samuel Walworth.*' He gave land at Barnsbury and at Wilton, co. Wilts, to Nathan Walworth, who thus endorses the deed, "my cosin Sam: deed of gift febr. 23 1637." Nathan does not mention this property in his Will, but later on he devises a tenement in New Sarum to the feoffees of Ringley school, which endowment seems to have lapsed, as it is not mentioned in the statement of revenue made in 1717. (See No. 64.) This tenement in New Sarum was probably identical with a house on the south side of the Market Place in Salisbury, purchased in 1594 by Ralph Walworth, which subsequently came into the possession of Nathan Walworth, as the deeds relating to the sale are preserved with other documents relating to the endowment of Ringley Chapel.

[49] '*Sir Matthew Lyster.*' Matthew Lister of Thornton, in Craven, whose career much resembles that of the late Sir Henry Holland, was educated at Oxford, where he became fellow of Oriel. After travelling abroad and taking a medical degree at Basle, he was made Physician to Queen Anne of Denmark, probably through the influence of Lady Pembroke, who must have known his family, and at whose house no doubt he became acquainted with Nathan Walworth. He was knighted by Charles I. and ultimately became President of the College of Physicians. He lived to be 92, "an instance of a constitution which either needed not the aid of his own faculty or proved their efficacy." (See Whitaker's *Hist. of Craven.*)

[50] '*Philoclea and Pamela and the Spawe.*' Philoclea and Pamela were the heroines of Sir Philip Sidney's *Arcadia*, a work probably well known to Nathan, as Sir Philip was Lord Pembroke's uncle. *The Spawe* was probably a view of Spa-fields, or Ducking-pond fields in Clerkenwell.

O

loving freind Sir Thomas Morgan[51] knight a stone pott or jugge
with cover and foot of silver-guilt   To Mr. John Bradle of Cat-
worth co. Hunt a silver slip spoon   To the right worll my very
good freind the Lo: Hungerford[52] a round mazer cupp with a
long foote of silver guilt   To Richard Shropshire five pounds
and my best grey suite lined with silk and silver lace both doub-
let hose and cloake and girdle which I usually weare with the
same suite and a pair of watchet silk stockins and garters suitable
and my sword and the picture of my late Lord and Master William earl of Pembroke   To John Harris five pounds and all my
stone bottles and jugges   To Mr. Fishe Proctor of the Arches
my large chess-board black and white   To Morgan Powley a
Purslaine Boule with a foot and cover of silver-guilt   To Alexander Hidden my cross-bowe Gaffle [?] and Arrowes   To Mistress
Joslyn a spur-royall   To the Minister of the Parish where I die
20ˢ and to the Poor there 40ˢ   To the Minister of the Parish of
Prestwich where I was born 20ˢ and to the Poor there 40ˢ

> After enumerating nearly 60 further bequests of small sums
> the testator recites the building and endowment of Ringley
> chapel and the appointment of feoffees [see No. 62] and
> thus proceeds :

I do hereby devise to the said feoffees all that my messuage
or tenement in New Sarum co. Wilts now or late in the occupation of Henry Rolfe upon trust that the said trustees shall employ the rents thereof for the better maintenance of the said
Preacher   And Whereas I have lately built a schoolhouse near
to the said Chappell I hereby will the said house to the said
Trustees their heirs and assigns for ever upon trust that the said
house shall be employed for a School and for the residence of a

---

[51] '*Sir Thomas Morgan.*' Possibly this was Sir Thomas Morgan, Knt., of Langs-
ton, high sheriff of Monmouthshire in 1637 ; but the *State Papers* mention another Sir
Thomas Morgan, probably a city knight, to whom the Treasury owed a large sum of
money in 1635.   (*State Papers*, Dom. series.)

[52] Ferdinando Lord Hungerford succeeded his father, in 1643, as sixth earl of
Huntingdon ; he married Lucy, daughter and heiress of Sir John Davies of Englefield,
and died in 1655.

School-master   And I hereby devise to the said trustees all my two oxgangs of land within the town of Flambro' co. York upon trust that the said trustees shall employ the yearly rents for the repairing of the said house and for the maintenance of an able and honest Schoolmaster to be named by the said Rectors of Prestwich Bury and Middleton or the greater number of them And my will is that the children within the Chappelry shall be freely taught without paying anything   The residue of all my goods chattells and hereditts I bequeath to my said loving nephew Nathan Walworth

Witnesses to Will

MICHAELL SAMSON
THOMAS JOHNSON
GEORGE HARDMAN
EDWARD POTHUIN

LXIV.— *A note of the Contributors to Mr. Holland*[53] *from midsomer* 1652 *to midsomer* 1653.

	£	s.	d.		£	s.	d.
Widowe Barrt		10	00	Peter Seddon Senr..			
Thomas Walworth[54].		04	00	Peter Seddon Junr..	01	01	08
John Walworth		10	00	Thomas Tildesley...		02	00
Ellis Fletcher.........		02	00	Alice Tildesley		01	00
Roger Dixon				Lawrence Rydeings.		01	00
Ioshua Dixon.........		02	00	Deborah Allens......		02	00
William Smith		04	00	Widowe Fletcher ...		07	00
Widowe Lomaxe ...		05	00	George Allens		05	00
Thomas Scoales ...		02	00	Thomas Seddon ...		06	08
Robert Answorth ...		02	00	Ellis Farnworth......		04	08
Thomas Heape[55] ...		07	00	Widowe Farnworth..		03	04
Richard Heape		04	00	Adam Thorpe		01	00
Richard Smethurst..		3		Iames Sharples		00	06
Widowe Ouldam ...		02	00	Edward Lomax......		00	06

£ s. d.
05 13 04

---

[53] '*Mr. Holland.*'   Then minister at Ringley.   The Presbyterians had raised the

LXV.— *Abstract of a Statement of the Revenue of Ringley Chapel dated June 13th 1717.*

The Statement recites the building and consecration of Ringley Chapel, the endowment of land in Little Benton before mentioned [No. 61] and the provision for the election of fresh Trustees from time to time and thus continues

Which course hath been observed and Nathan Mort of Wharton Hall within Tildsley co. Lanc. gentleman William Wilson[56] of Poppithorne in the same county Gentleman Iames Seddon[57] of Prestolee in the same county yeoman and Robt Bolton of Kersley

---

endowment of the chapel from 16*l.* to 40*l.* in 1650, by applying part of the tythes of Kirkham to that purpose, but it is probable that the money was irregularly paid, and that a voluntary contribution was needed. Thomas Holland, M.A., of the University of Edinburgh, took the covenant in 1647, having received a call to Ringley. He removed to Blackley in 1653, was ejected in 1662. and retired to Oldham, where he died in 1675, aged 57. Calamy says, he was connected with the Hollands of Denton, but I have not been able to identify him. Perhaps he belonged to the Hollands of Rhodes, who descended from the same stock as the Denton family. From Richard Holland, elder son of Thurstan de Holland (who acquired the estate at Denton, through his mother), descended the Hollands of Denton and Heaton. From William, younger son of Thurstan, descended the Hollands of Clifton, through his marriage with Marjery, daughter of Henry de Trafford. About the middle of the sixteenth century, William Holland of Clifton, and John Foxe of Latham, married the two daughters and co-heiresses of —— Parr of Rhodes, and divided the estate between them ; and at the beginning of this century, Holland Watson, the grandson of William Holland of Rhodes (who died in 1739), possessed half of Rhodes, while the descendants of John Foxe possessed the other half (see Gregson's *Portfolio*, p. 208, and Mr. Langton's note to *Towneley's Inquisitions*, vol. ii, p. 135).

[54] '*Thomas Walworth*' of Ringley, a witness in the Will of 'neighbour' Peter, proved in 1664. In May 1656 he married, at Prestwich, Anne, daughter of John Siddall of Whitefield. He died July 1671, and was buried at Prestwich.

[55] '*Thomas Heape*' of Pilkington, married (at Manchester, January 1623-4) Anne, daughter of John Foxe of the Rhodes, steward to William, earl of Derby.

[56] '*William Wilson.*' See No. 25, and note.

[57] '*Iames Seddon*,' grandson of 'neighbour' Peter. In his Will, proved January 1721, he settled his land in Kersley, Farnworth, and Salford, and his 'feudment' in Pilkington, on his eldest son William, and mentioned as his 'kinsman,' George Seddon, the great-grandfather of Thomas Seddon the painter, whose picture of Jerusalem is in the National Gallery.

in the same county yeoman now are intitled to the premises in Trust for the use of the Minister of the said Chapel

The same Trustees are likewise intitled under the Gift of the said Nathan Walwork to the Reversion and Inheritance of a certain Messuage and Tenement in Sharples in the said county of Lancaster and of a yearly rent of Twenty shillings and Tenpence issuing out of the same Tenement and reserved by Lease made thereof before the founding of the said Chapel for a long term whereof eighty years or upwards are yet in being

About fifteen or twenty years after the Consecration of the said Chapel the Inhabitants of Ringley Outwood Kersley Clifton and others charitably disposed erected an House and suitable Outhousing for the use of the said Minister of the said Chapel which together with two gardens thereunto belonging are now occupied and enjoyed accordingly

Iohn Starkie late of Huntroid co. Lanc. Esquire by Indenture of Lease dated the 10th of December 1668 Demised unto William Hulme of Kersley[58] aforesaid a certain Plott of wast ground in Kersley of about 50 yards in length and 20 yards in breadth whereupon the said William Hulme then agreed to build and hath since built an house and some outbuildings for ffive hundred years next after the date of the same lease under the yearly rent of Fourpence payable to the said Mr Starkie and his heirs and the said lease declares that the Rent profit and income of the said Parcel of land and building shall be disbursed and paid by the said William Hulme and his Executors and Assigns for the Use of the Minister of Ringley aforesaid which hath been accordingly done to this time and William Baguley Gentleman Executor of the said Mr Hulme is intitled to the said Lease and Term of the same Premises which Premises are all the Estate belonging to the said Chapel

---

[58] '*William Hulme,*' the Founder of the Hulmeian Exhibitions, left, in his Will, 5*l.* to "Joshua Dixon clerke, whom I desire to preach my funerall sermon."

And this is further to Certify that the said six⎫
Oxgangs of land and all other the Premisses in ⎪
Benton co. York lie distant from the said Chapel ⎪
80 long miles or upwards and are now lett at £24 ⎬ £24   0   0
per ann. and the housing is very ruinous by Age ⎪
and Materials of Buildings are very scarce and ⎪
dear in that country and great deductions must be ⎪
made thereout on that and other accounts .... ⎭

That the said Sharples rent is £1   0 10

That the said Chapel House and Gardens are of
about the yearly value of £2   0   0

That the said House Outhousing and Plott of land
in Kersley is of about of the yearly value of £3 10   0

In the whole amounting to............................. £30 10 10

And lastly that the said Chapel is situate in a Country village
150 miles from London and Three miles from the Parish or
Mother church of Prestwich Three miles from the Parish church
of Bolton and Three miles from the Parish church of Radcliffe
and there is none other church or chapel with three miles thereof

All which is humbly certified this 13th day of Iune A.D. 1717 by

IOSH. DIXON Minister of Ringley.

Attested upon Oath by Wm̄ Wilson and Iames Seddon before
us   RIC. WROE[59] Warden⎫
                      of Manchester   ⎪
                      ROGʳ. BOLTON   ⎬Commissioners.
                      ROBT ASHETON   ⎭

Witness our Hands
        WM. WILSON
        IAMES SEDDON

59 'Ric. Wroe,' born at Heaton Gate, in Prestwich, in 1641. He became warden
of Manchester in 1684, and died in 1718, aged 76.

LXVI.— *Deed of partition of lands in Kersley dated March the 23rd 1597.*

To all christian people to whome these presents shall come, or the same shall see heare reade or understand. The Right hon^ble William Earle of Darbie[60] sendeth greetinge in our lord god everlastinge. Wheras I the said Earle and George Hulton Esquyer,[61] and Raphe Seddon[62] doe howld certaine howslinge lands Tenem^ts and hereditame^ts in Kyrsley w^thin the Cowntie of Lanc his [as?] Tenñts in Comon and undevyded; For the devydinge severinge and particõn of wch lands and hereditam^ts that is to saie to devyde and part the lands of myne inheritance from the lands and hereditam^ts of the said George Hulton and Raphe Seddon in Kyrsley aforesaid. Knowe yee me the said Earle to have authorized constituted and appoynted and by these presents doe authorize constitute and appoynt my trustie and welbeloved servants Edward Warren[63] and William Orrell[64] Esquyers and Francis Holt[65] gent. and my welbeloved Robt Hyde Esquyer,

[60] '*Earle of Darbie.*' The sixth earl, who succeeded his brother Ferdinando in 1595.

[61] '*George Hulton*' of Farnworth, who married Margaret, fourth daughter of Robert Hyde of Hyde and Norbury, and died before February 1613.

[62] '*Raphe Seddon,*' the father of 'neighbour' Peter. He died February 10th 1611-12, and in his Will appointed his brother-in-law, John Foxe, and Alexander Horrocks, vicar of Deane, overseers, and his wife Mary, and his eldest son Peter, his executors. Raphe Seddon inherited this land through his mother Cicely, younger daughter of Thomas Seddon of Kersley, who devised his land there to his two daughters, Cicely and Eliz., wife of Thomas Marcroft. This deed did not end the dispute, for two years later George Hulton went to law with Raphe Seddon and others as to lands and "digging coals" at Pilkington Manor and Kyrsley (see the *Calendar to Pleadings*). I may mention here that the Seddon arms (see end of vol.) are those borne by John Strettell Seddon, Esq., the nephew and representative of James Seddon of Prestolee, who died in 1846. Some of the Seddons had "non sono, sed dono," for their motto. James Seddon himself preferred "Dictum, factum," as though his name was spelled "Said, done," and implied that his word was as good as his bond.

[63] '*Edward Warren,*' son of John Warren of Poynton, in the county of Chester, and Margaret, daughter of Sir Richard Molineux of Sefton.

[64] '*William Orrell*' of Turton, in the county of Lancaster.

[65] '*Francis Holt*' of Gristlehurst, in the county of Lancaster, who married Catherine, daughter of William Ashton of Clegg (Dugdale).

Samnel Hyde and Eyles Ainesworth[66] gent or any towe of them, whereof the said Edw: Warren, Willm Orrell or Francis Holt to be one, and the said Robt Hyde, Samuel Hyde or Eyles Aynsworth to be an other to Survaie all and everye the said lands and hereditam^ts in Kyrslcy aforesaid, and to devyde sever and make partiĉon of the howsinge lands and hereditam^ts of myne inheritance from the howslinge lands and hereditam^ts of the said George Hulton and Raphe Seddon ratablie and proporconablie accordinge to the rate and proporcon of everye mans anncyent rents and Services in such mañr. and forme as to my said Comissioner or such towe of them as aforesaid shalbe thought most reasonable and indifferent. And I the said Earle doe by these presents Ratyfie approve and allowe all and whatsoever my said Commissioner or such towe of them as aforesaid shall doe in or about the due execuĉon of the premisses as fully and whollie and in as ample and large manner and forme as y^t I the said Earle were personalye present at the doeinge therof. In wytnes wherof I the said Earle have hereunto putt my hand and Seale the xxiij^th day of Marche 1597 Anno Rē. Elizabeth Quadragisimo

Subscrybed

ROBERT HYDE   WILL: DERBY.
SAMNEL HYDE

LXVII.— *Abstract of Indenture between Raphe Seddon of Pilkington and William Potts of Bury.*[67]

Indenture made the 5th day of September 5th Iames 1st (1607) between Raphe Seddon of Pilkington co. Lancaster gentleman of the one part and William Potts of Burie gent of the other part witnesseth that Raphe Seddon had demysed set and to farm letten unto the said William Potts all that his fourth part and

---

[66] '*Eyles Ainesworth,*' one of the Ainsworths of Plessington. In 1574 he furnished, in the general muster of soldiers, "1 coat of plate, 1 long-bow, 1 sheffe of arrows, 1 caliver, 1 skull, 1 bill (Foster's *Lanc. Pedigrees*).

[67] Communicated to *Local Gleanings* by W. A. Abram, Esq.

purpurtie of one messuage and tenement situate in Manchester co. Lane at the corner of a streete there called the Hanging Ditche late in the tenure of Stephen Browne of Manchester gent betwixt the lands of Robert Radcliff gent now in the tenure of Iames Houghe upon the South parte and the higheway that leadeth to Newton lane on the North Easte parte the which said Burgage garden and premises the said Raphe Seddon doth hold in common with William Hardman and Thomas Marcroft[68] as in the right of Elizabeth his late wife deceased to have and to hold the said fourth part of the said premises for the natural lives of him the said William Potts Edward Potts son of Edward Potts of Cambridge gent and Iohn Crompton son of Iohn Crompton the younger of Pilkington yeoman and during the life of the longest liver of them paying yearly to Raphe Seddon sixteen shillings at the feast days of the birth of our Lord God and the Nativity of St. Iohn the Baptist .

Witnesses Robert Syddall Iohn Crompton Martin Cundlyfe Robert Leighe Robert Leighe the younger

---

[68] ' *Thomas Marcroft,*' married Eliz., elder daughter of Thomas Seddon of Kyrsley, and obtained with his wife land in Kersley and Farnworth, which his son, Robert, afterwards sold to Ralph Assheton, Esq., of Great Lever. (Barritt *MSS.*)

stolee.

ughter of Peter Standish of Erley, by Alice, daughter of Richard
, and grand-daughter of John Radford, lord of Kyrsley, *temp.*
II. (*Barritt MSS.* in Chetham Library).

Kyrsley.⚭

f Kyrsley.⚭

of Kyrsley,⚭
1553.

ly Seddon.⚭Peter Seddon of Prestolee, in the Outwood of Pilkington,
ied before | in the county of Lancaster, witness to deed of Gilbert
(*Cal. to* | Hyndeley of Hyndeley, 12 June 1541; died before 7 April
dings). | 1575 (*Manchester Court Leet Records*).

on of Pilkington,⚭Eliza, daughter of   A Daughter,
hew, Peter, sole —— Rothwell,   who married John Heywood
his Will, proved married at Eccles,   of Bolton, in the county of
1639.   January 1592.   ·   Lancaster, *temp.* Edw. VI.

PETER SEDDON of PRESTO   Dorothy Seddon,⚭William Hulton, eldest   Thomas Seddon.
(*Court Leet Records*); friend a   married at Prest- | son of George Hulton   Married Maria Walw
of Nathan Walworth, origina   wich 10th Feb- | of Farnworth; baptized   at Prestwich, Nover
ley chapel and school; inte   ruary 1624. | at Bolton July 1594.   1651; interred there
15th February 1663-4; Will   December 1670.
ter March 1664 (see Tombst

Peter Seddon of   Robert Seddon.   Mary.
baptized at Prest. A. of Christ's College, Cambridge; vicar of Langley, in the   Anna.
captain in the Pa ounty of Derby; baptized at Prestwich October 1629; interred   Esther.
1696.   t Ringley March 1695-6 (see Tombstone).

of Prestolee,⚭Deborah, daughter of ——   John Seddon.
rred at Ring- | Unsworth of Whitfield;   Baptized at Prestwich
1655; ir   1726 (see | married at Prestwich 1st   11th November 1652.
1720; ii | January 1682; interred at
ary 172 | Ringley October 1699.
Salford,
on son mas Seddon of Prestolee.⚭Ellen, daughter of ——
lized at Prestwich 10th | Smith of Hindley; born
ust 1684; interred at | 1685; married at Wigan
ley 11th November 1744; | 1722; interred at Ring-
c proved at Chester May | ley 26th August 1758.
J; trustee of Ringley
el.

Joseph Seddon.⚭   . Their   Thomas Seddon of Prestolee,⚭Mary, daughter of Williai
Baptized at Ringley 30th | married   only son; born 17th November 1727; | of Eccles, married there N
March 1730.   of Kers-   interred at Ringley July 1776.   interred February 1793.

Eliz. Seddon.⚭(S   of
Married at Man-   m ,⚭Margaret, daughter of Elias   Ellen Seddon,⚭John Kelsall of
chester August   of l Chadwick of Wigan, interred   married at Mottram | ob. 29th July 18
1806.   of at Ringley 24th June 1823.   3rd Novemb. 1794.

James Seddon of Pres y, daughter of Robert   Ellen Seddon,   Elias Chadwick of Pudleston,
Born 22nd June 1792; ii atherall of Liverpool,   born 20th Jan-   county of Hereford. J.P.;
Ringley December 1846 rred at Ringley Feb-   uary 1808; ob.   Sheriff 1854: ob. July 1875.
of Ringley chapel, and y 1860.   6th February
the school; ob. *s.p.*   1871.

The Family of Peter Seddon of Prestolee.

Richard Seddon. Held lands in Kyrsley in Farnworth, in the county of Lancaster, of Thomas West, lord of Mancester, 1st May 1473 (*Harl. MSS.*, cod. 2112, fol. 106). == Jonn, daughter of Peter Standish of Erley, by Alice, daughter of Richard Radford, and grand-daughter of John Radford, lord of Kyrsley, *temp.* Richard II. (*Barritt MSS.* in Chetham Library).

Giles Seddon of Kyrsley.

Raphe Seddon of Kyrsley.

Thomas Seddon of Kyrsley, deceased before 1553.

Thomas Marcroft. == Eliz. Seddon. Their son, Robert, Hold land in Salforde in 1552 sold his land in Kyrsley to Raphe (*Col. to Plead.*, 1 Mary, vol. i., Asherton, Esq., of Great Lever. p. 479).

Carly Seddon. == Peter Seddon of Prestolee, in the Outwood of Pilkington. Married before in the county of Lancaster, witness to deed of Gilbert 1553 (*Col. to* Hyndeley of Hyndeley, 12 June 1541; died before 7 April *Pleadings*. 1575 (*Manchester Court Leet Records*).

Raphe Seddon of Prestolee — eldest son == Mary, eldest daughter of (*Court Leet Records*), legatee and executor William Fose of the tor of William Fose in Will proved at Rholes, in Pilkington, Chester, June 1590; held land in Kyrsley 1597, and in Hanging Ditch, Manchester, September 1607; Will proved; May 1611. == William Fose of the Rholes, in Pilkington, clerk comptroller to Henry, Earl of Derby.

Michael Seddon of Pilkington, left his nephew, Peter, sole executor in his Will, proved at Chester in 1637.

Ellen, daughter of — Rothwell, married at Eccles, January 1592.

A Daughter, who married John Heywood of Ilchoat, in the county of Lancaster, *temp.* Edw. VI.

Peter Seddon of Prestolee, eldest son == Ellen, daughter of William Seddon, (*Court Leet Records*), friend and correspondent of Nathan Walworth, assigned trustee of Ringley chapel and school; interred at Ringley, 1st December 1643. Will proved at Chester March 1664 (see Tombstone). == Ellen, daughter of William Seddon, who left her £200 in Will dated February 1653; married at Prestwich.

William Seddon, M.A. == Katharine, daughter of Magd. Coll., Cam-, of —, interred at bridge; rector of Graspridge, in the county of Cheshire; interred three 8th September 1671.

Dorothy Seddon, married at Prestwich, 10th Feb. 1624.

William Hulton, eldest son of George Hulton of Farnworth; baptised at Todon July 1594.

Thomas Seddon. Married Maria Walworth at Prestwich, November 1651; interred there 9th December 1670.

Peter Seddon of Prestolee, eldest son == Lunice, daughter baptised at Prestwich 6th April 1617; of — interred captain in the Parliament army; living at Prestwich, January 1673.

Ralph Seddon, second son, 1674; Will proved 1675, left issue.

John Seddon, Captain in Royal army, January 1642.

Robert Seddon, M.A. of Christ's College, Cambridge; vicar of Langley, in the county of Derby; baptised at Prestwich October 1629; interred at Ringley March 1705 (see Tombstone).

Mary. Anne. Esther.

James Seddon of Prestolee. == Martha, daughter of Baptised at Prestwich 23rd November — ; interred at 1655; interred at Ringley November Ringley May 1731. 1720; in Will, proved at Chester January 1721, settled land in Kyrsley and Salford, and "feoffment" in Pilkington on son William.

Peter Seddon, born 1646; interred at Ringley 1740.

Robert Seddon of Prestolee, born 1658; interred at Ringley September 1726 (see Tombstone).

Deborah, daughter of — Unsworth of Whitfield; married at Prestwich 1st January 1684; interred at Ringley October 1709.

John Seddon. Baptised at Prestwich 11th November 1672.

William Seddon of Prestolee. == Anne, daughter of Baptised at Prestwich 23rd —; interred at chapel; interred there 21st January 1707.

John. Peter. James.

Thomas Seddon of Prestolee. Ellen, daughter of Baptised at Prestwich 10th South of Hindley; born August 1684; interred at 1685; married in Wigan Wigan 11th November 1744; 1722; interred at Ringley Will proved at Chester May October 1709. 1745; trustee of Ringley chapel.

Joseph Seddon. Baptised at Ringley 30th March 1730.

Peter Seddon, second son, == Jane, daughter of — baptised at Ringley June interred at Ringley 24th 1735; interred March 1820. September 1818.

Ellen. James. John.

Anne Seddon. Born 1723; interred at Prestwich June 1770.

William Xing. == Their daughter Ellen married Egerton Crowe of Kersley Hall.

Thomas Seddon of Prestolee, only son; born 13th November 1737; of Kceles, interred at Ringley July 1770.

Mary, daughter of William Stretell; married there May 1751; interred February 1703.

Eliz. Seddon. (Second wife.) == George Scholes. Married at Manor of High Bank, Prestwich, who Chester August —; interred, first, Harriet, daughter 1800. —, of Helland Walson, Esq., J.P.

Robert Seddon of Prestolee. Baptised at Ringley March 1756; interred at Ringley December 1810.

Thomas Seddon of Prestolee, born 21st November 1760; interred at Ringley 24th November 1820.

Margaret, daughter of Elias Chadwick of Wigan, interred at Ringley 29th June 1823.

Ellen Seddon. == John Keshall of Ardwick, married at Mottram 6th 29th July 1828. 3rd November 1794.

James Seddon of Prestolee. Born 23rd June 1762; interred at Ringley December 1809; trustee of Ringley chapel, and endowed the school; ob. s.p.

Robert Seddon of Pendleton. Born 11th October 1764; interred at Ringley 13th November 1801; ob. s.p.

Eliza Seddon. Interred at Ringley August 1848.

Sutetsell Seddon of Fairfield. == Mary, daughter of Robert West Derby; born 10th April Wenthorall of Liverpool, 1806; interred at Ringley 9th interred at Ringley Feb- June 1862. ruary 1800.

Ellen Seddon, born 20th January 1848; ob. 6th February 1871.

Ellen Chadwick of Pailhoton, in the county of Hereford, J.P.; High Sheriff 1854; ob. July 1871.

INDEX.

INDEX.

CHARLES SIMMS AND CO., PRINTERS, MANCHESTER.

ERRATA.

Page viii, line 12, *for* "Sir Thomas Lyster," *read* "Sir Matthew Lyster."

,,   ix,   ,,   20, *for* "Old Hull," *read* "Old Hall."

,,   xiii, ,,   6, *for* "1569," *read* "1659."

,,   11,   ,,   13, *for* "venuint," *read* "veniunt."

,,   14, last line, *for* "Sir John," *read* "John."

,,   40, line 11, *for* "Pertia," *read* "Tertia."

,,   87, last line but one, *for* "stipend-wages was," *read* "stipend-wages were."

138543

www.ingramcontent.com/pod-product-compliance
Lightning Source LLC
Chambersburg PA
CBHW020548270326
41927CB00006B/769